You are Not Alone

My Experience with Postpartum Depression

Michelle Habrych

Front cover design by Faith Ricci, back cover design by Brent Habrych

ISBN Print 979-8-9871649-0-7 ebook 979-8-9871649-1-4

Typesetting by autograph.pub

For Krista

Table of Contents

Preface XV

Introduction XXIII

1. My story begins I

2. Not alone 5

3. Control 9

4. Focus on the positive II

5. Asking for help I5

6. Breaking through the numbness I7

7. Celebrate small victories 2I

8. Finding comfort 25

9. Confidence beyond circumstances 27

10. The snowball effect 29

11. No record of wrongs 33

12. More to my life 37

13. Feeling desperate 39

14. Thoughts and grief 43

15. The power of love 47

16. Longing for more 5I

17. Knowledge empowers 53

18. Household help 55

19. Confront and feel emotions 57

20. Good and bad days 61

21. Shared experience 63

22. Visual reminder 65

23. Accepting assistance 69

24. Managing anger 71

25. Get out! 73

26. Seek support 77

27. Extrovert or introvert? 81

28. Communication is key 85

29. Depressed dad? 89

30. Future thoughts 91

31. Desperate measures 93

32. Bring it all in prayer 97

33. Noticing changes 99

34. Dealing with discouragement 101

35. Understand what you can control ... 103

36. Handling disappointment 107

37. Reaching out 109

38. Mentioning medication 111

39. Meditate on God's Word 113

40. Change is hard 115

41. Write daily goals 117

42. Being intentional 119

43. Choosing to communicate 121

44. Cling to God 125

45. Try journaling 129

46. Problems with procrastination 131

47. Sleepless night 135

48. Anchored by faith 139

49. Big picture thinking 143

50. Avoid adding to your depression ... 147

51. Ready for revision 151

52. A loose schedule 155

53. Rest in God 157

54. Sweet slumber 159

55. God will use this 163

56. When setbacks arise 165

57. Examine your emotions 169

58. Bible study benefits 171

59. New perspective 173

60. No longer reacting 175

61. Trusting in trials 177

62. Appreciating my baby 179

63. Fear no evil 181

64. Joyful 185

65. Time for practical application 187

66. Hopeful 189

67. Make a list 191

68. Giving thanks 193

69. Identify bad habits 195

70. Continuing struggles 197

71. Excitement for life beyond PPD 199

72. Feeling better 203

73. Afterword 205

Appendix 207

Further Reading 215

Acknowledgements 219

About the Author 221

Foreword

As a mental health counselor specializing in the treatment of perinatal mental health disorders I sit and talk with many women navigating various types and stages of postpartum depression, anxiety, or OCD. One of the most pervasive things I hear from women walking through these experiences is the feeling of isolation. New mothers often feel fear, guilt, and shame about what is happening to them, which makes it difficult for them to reach out for support. This further perpetuates the isolation and darkness that encompasses.

I am so grateful that Michelle Habrych has so bravely decided to share her journey through postpartum depression in the format of a memoir. In this work she generously lets the reader into her home, her heart, her mind, her marriage struggles, and also her faith. What a gift she has provided. Through her writing she has become a companion to other women who may also be struggling.

Michelle gently shares her journey from pain and confusion, to the seeking and utilization of limited resources, and finally through her journey of accessing professional services to help her across the finish line of recovery. With her Christian faith as an anchor and a source of strength, Michelle embodies a reliance on Jesus through a most difficult and dark time. I have no doubt that this book will be a gift to many readers.

Michelle Schaefer, LCPC, PMH-C
Licensed Clinical Professional Counselor
Certified Perinatal Mental Health Provider

Foreword

Thirty-seven years ago, I believed I was an awful mother, a despicable person, and better off dead. What would make me think that? I was the mother of my third child, a beautiful baby boy, and I had slipped into the tarry black pit of postpartum depression. I spent a year in that dark hole unaware that it was an illness. Instead, I believed it was my own character flaws that were shaping my experience. When I found myself contemplating a plan to end the pain, by God's grace, I woke up to the fact that I desperately needed help.

So much more is known about PPD now. Much has been written and published. I'm so grateful for attentive doctors, good medications, and brave women like Michelle who will tell their stories and remind others that they are not alone. Help, hope and healing are possible and available. You, young mother, are so loved. You are a light that should not be dimmed by this terrible illness. Come out of the dark and enjoy the bright light of life and motherhood that you were meant for. I wish you health and joy! I found it, and you can, too!

Lynda Toner

Preface

Samantha sighed heavily as her infant started to cry yet again. When would this baby ever sleep? The new mother ached for relief from the tired haze she lived in daily. She knew she should be grateful to have a baby when some of her friends struggled to conceive, yet Samantha desperately longed to escape the hamster wheel of her life. Where were the magical moments the media portrayed of a blissful baby being rocked by a beautiful, smiling mama? She could not recall the last time she smiled. Maybe it was in the hospital when the doctor announced, "It's a girl!" The past few months were a blur.

The crying intensified. Her baby girl was not falling asleep as she was supposed to do at this time of day. All of the experts promised they could help if she did things their way. The whisperer's method, the wise baby technique, her mother's experience: Nothing was working.

This is not what I signed up for! she screamed in her mind, locking herself in the bathroom and turning on the fan to drown out the baby's cries. *I cannot pick her up again right now. I need a nap, too!*

A weary woman stared back at her in the dusty mirror: dark circles under her eyes, a messy ponytail on top of her head, spit-up stains on her bulky sweatshirt. *Who have I become?* she wondered.

Bone tired and sobbing, Samantha climbed into the bathtub and leaned her head back against the dry tiles. *What am I doing wrong? Why won't she sleep? I am such a failure. I should have never had a kid. What was I thinking?*

The thoughts in her weary mind started to spiral out of control. *I need to escape. If I can just get away, someone else can take better care of her than I can. I am the worst mother in the world.*

Stop it! another voice inside scolded Samantha. *Your husband will be home from work in an hour.*

Yes, she would just have to hold on a little bit longer. *Just a little bit longer,* she comforted herself, blowing her nose loudly into a wad of toilet paper, *then you can sleep.*

Does this scenario sound familiar? It's a partially fictionalized representation of my life when I experienced the surprising condition known medically as postpartum depression (PPD). I say surprising because I was completely caught off guard by the thoughts I was thinking and the emotions I was feeling, largely because I was relatively unfamiliar with postpartum depression. It was simply not on my radar.

Understanding postpartum depression and related diagnoses

I want to share my own personal story with you, but first let's bring some important facts into the light. Mood swings after giving birth are common for women. According to Postpartum Support International (PSI), as many as 80 percent experience weepiness as well as emotional instability in the first few weeks after delivery. This can be classified as "baby blues" and can actually begin just prior to the birth and continue for two to three weeks. It is marked by extreme emotional highs and lows. One minute a mom is loving her baby, the next she bursts into tears. This can result from the cascade of hormones in the body as a result of the pregnancy and delivery. Exhaustion due to sleep deprivation only compounds the situation. Baby blues are very common during this intense time, but it does not last long. Once the body stabilizes, baby blues typically resolves without aid from medical professionals. If things are not changing after three to four weeks, it may be postpartum depression.

Postpartum depression may begin before a woman gives birth and includes the period up to one year after. Symptoms include feelings of anger or irritability; lack of interest in the baby; appetite and sleep disturbance; crying and sadness; feelings of guilt, shame, or hopelessness; loss of interest, joy, or pleasure in the things you used to enjoy; and possible thoughts of harming the baby or yourself. These feelings may take as long as a year to manifest in a new mother, yet it is still considered postpartum depression. PSI says postpartum depression may affect as high as 15 percent of women after they give birth. It is temporary and treatable with help from medical professionals.

A new mother experiencing symptoms of anxiety related to the baby and having intrusive thoughts may be diagnosed with postpartum anxiety. A new mother may experience this with or without depression. Some symptoms include constant worry or feelings of dread, racing thoughts, inability to sit still, sleep and appetite disturbances, dizziness, hot flashes, and nausea. This is also treatable, and you should seek professional assistance to get through it.

Postpartum obsessive compulsive disorder (OCD) is another related diagnosis, one that is greatly misunderstood. Symptoms of this include obsessions, which are thoughts or mental images related to the baby. The thoughts can be very frightening and disturbing to a new mother, so she fears what might happen if she shares them with someone else. Bonding with the baby may be disrupted as the overwhelming fear of acting on these ideas terrifies the woman. If you are thinking about things that are out of character for you, perhaps even questioning "what kind of monster am I?" after having such thoughts, seek professional help. This is more common than most women realize, and it is very treatable.

Only two in 1000 women experience the condition classified as postpartum psychosis, which is not a level of postpartum depression yet is often confused with the term. Instead, postpartum psychosis is related to mania, in the family of bipolar disorders. A woman with postpartum psychosis may experience sleep disruption as well as hallucinations and delusions. These delusions will vary greatly from her normal experience prior to this time. She can be paranoid, refuse to eat, have extreme agitation, or experience thoughts which make her want to harm herself or her baby, but she is not necessarily upset by these ideas. This is what is usually shown on the news because the media highlights sensational stories. Postpartum psychosis is considered a medical emergency. If you are experiencing any of those thoughts, feelings, or hallucinations, please stop reading right now and seek immediate medical help from local medical staff at 911. Alternatively, call The National Suicide Prevention Lifeline at 988 or 1-800-273-8255. Do not delay; call now or go to your local emergency room for an evaluation. Medical professionals report success with treating postpartum psychosis by medical means.

To find out more about these different conditions, there is also the National Maternal Mental Health Hotline which you can call or text 24 hours a day, seven days a week. It is 1-833-943-5746. This hotline is staffed by professional providers trained specifically to assess and support postpartum moms. PSI also offers a non-emergency helpline at 1-800-944-4773.

If you are feeling "the blues" but they are getting worse and you cannot think clearly, or you feel very alone as a new mother, please read on. I have been there, and I am writing to tell you, "You are not alone." When I encountered PPD, feelings of being alone were the prevailing lies whispered in my ear and echoing in my soul. I wrote this book because God called me to share with you my experience (you can read more about this in the Afterword). Throughout this book, I include scripture verses which encouraged me during my depression or which I feel may inspire you as you read. I pray that in reading my story and reflections on it, you will have a new hope, gain comfort, and experience a peace that transcends all understanding.

"Therefore, since we have been justified through faith, we have peace with God through our Lord Jesus Christ, through whom we have gained access by faith into this grace in which we now stand. And we boast in the hope of the glory of God." (Romans 5:1-2)

"And the peace of God, which transcends all understanding, will guard your hearts and minds in Christ Jesus." (Philippians 4:7)

Introduction

In 2003, I gave birth to my second child. The weeks that followed were kind of a blur, but I do recall that I was angry and sad. I desperately wanted to escape the pit into which I was sinking. I felt as if I were slipping away from a life that I remembered into one that belonged to someone else. A friend expressed concern that I may be experiencing something a little more than the baby blues. I thought, *Okay, I'll look it up. What could that mean anyway?*

I found and took an online quiz. *Ding ding ding! You have postpartum depression!* Well, maybe that's not what it said, but it sure felt that way. While it was good to have a label for the way I was feeling, it was also scary. Did that mean I was going to try to kill my kids? Would I be in a slump forever? Surely Christians can't experience depression, can they?

There were so many unknowns and misconceptions. I'm a reader and a trained journalist, so I sought out material on the subject. In the moments when I could think more clearly, I read everything I could find to investigate the self-diagnosis.

Accepting that I was feeling this way was one part of the puzzle. Doing something about it was entirely different. Our family was between health insurance policies at the time. My husband, Brent, preferred that I not do or say anything to mess up our application for private insurance or get labeled with a pre-existing condition; this was years prior to the changes in insurance laws. Therefore, I could not seek professional medical help in the way that I might otherwise have done. (In light of changes to the law, I advise you to find help as soon as possible if you are feeling depressed.) I did seek counseling and support groups, though. I also continued reading and I journaled all the time. These journals now serve to help me recall my experiences back then, because I do not remember much from that year.

So many things may have contributed to the postpartum depression I suffered. What does that matter, though, when you're in the midst of it? Does having something or someone to blame change the situation? Would naming a reason for my depression relieve the guilt of feeling anything less than happy after my child was born? It definitely was not what I expected. Honestly, it was a living hell.

Compelled to share my experience, I wrote this memoir to provide encouragement for those going through it. There are not enough resources to help young mothers and their families understand postpartum depression. I open my heart to you in order to dispel the myths and misconceptions. My deep desire is to provide hope for families with a loved one experiencing postpartum depression. There is still a soft spot in my heart for young mothers in the fog after childbirth. I pray my words can provide support to remind you that you are not alone.

The format of this book is short excerpts from my journals (signified by a date and change in font), followed by reflection, words of encouragement, scripture verses, and questions for you to consider or challenges to take action towards your own healing. The entries may be read quickly in order, as you would read any book, or slowly, as a daily devotional to help you in the spare moments in which you have quiet time to read. I hope you consider this book as a friend who has been through what you're experiencing, written just for you.

Please note: All names of those outside of my family have been changed. Also, as I was writing in my journal, I did not describe who each person was, often only using their names. It's unimportant to keep track of these specific people as you might characters in a novel. The main people to remember are Brent, my husband; Jesse, my toddler, and Anastasia (Ana), my baby.

My story begins

In some ways, I feel like my entire second pregnancy was a setup for what I experienced. I was the fairly new mother of a sweet baby boy, Jesse. He and I were getting into a rhythm. I finally was taking control of my health and losing weight. I cannot remember how much I lost, but it was significant. Then, the week before his first birthday party in May 2002, I found out I was expecting again. To say I was happy about the timing would be a lie. I was not planning to have children so close in age, and I felt that being pregnant would undo all of my hardwon health gains. I told myself I would continue to eat healthily and exercise to minimize my pregnancy weight gain. While my intentions were honorable, I found that I was unable to keep that commitment to myself, gaining not only excessive weight but the guilt that comes along with it.

As the pregnancy progressed, my OB-GYN was concerned about my blood pressure. I experienced high blood pressure prior to pregnancy, so this was not unexpected, but it was frustrating. I went in for regular tests, and I was told to be on bedrest. Try doing that with a toddler who isn't walking very much on his own! To make attending my weekly check-ups easier, a good friend was watching my son at her house with her own young daughter. At an appointment in early January a few weeks before my due date, the OB-GYN unexpectedly said to me, "What are you doing tonight? Want to have a baby?"

Shocked? So was I. I had just told my son I would see him soon, and now instead I was headed to the hospital. My husband joined me there as I mentally prepared to experience induced labor yet again. The OB-GYN had induced labor for my first baby's delivery due to my blood pressure concerns, and here we were one more time. It was disappointing not to have the opportunity to go into labor on my own. So many women had stories to tell about it while I had, "Well, my doctor hooked me up to a machine administering pitocin and eventually the contractions started..."

It was a long night in labor and delivery. At least I knew a little more of what to expect this time. Only 19 months earlier I had been in a similar situation. This time, thankfully, the labor was a few hours shorter. In the early morning hours, my contractions were starting to get stronger, and I asked for the epidural. I recall that my nurse was having trouble contacting my OB-GYN, or maybe the anesthesiologist could not get in there. Whichever the case, when the shot was finally administered, during which I continued to have a lot of contractions, it turned out to be too late for the drugs to be of any help. The OB-GYN pronounced that I was dilated to 10 and needed to start pushing. Every moment of the delivery was felt intensely. Then, about a half hour after the birth of my daughter, Anastasia, the drugs kicked in and I was physically numb.

That pain and subsequent numbness actually foreshadowed what was to come. We were in a hurry to get home to our son, so it's likely that we requested an earlier release. Breastfeeding was going smoothly and everything looked good, so we were permitted to leave. That same week, however, the pediatrician noticed my daughter's bilirubin count was high, causing her to have yellowish skin (a condition known as jaundice). The doctor prescribed phototherapy to bring it down, so she slept wrapped in a special blanket. We called her our little glow worm.

Soon after that, the pain started for me. It was beyond cramps, beyond contractions. We rushed back to the hospital where it was discovered I had some kind of infection in my uterus. The doctors were going to do a D&C (dilation and curettage, a surgical procedure in which the cervix is dilated to scrape the uterine lining and remove abnormal tissues) and put me on some strong medications. I still desired to continue breastfeeding my newborn, but we were told my daughter would not be permitted to stay in my hospital room with me overnight. Instead, I would "pump and dump" at the hospital to keep my milk flowing. My husband would have to give her formula while I was in the hospital for 24 to 48 hours.

For a day, maybe two— the time is lost to my memory— my husband did nothing at home except take care of our glow worm and our toddler. My D&C was successful and I recovered well, but it was yet another "it's not supposed to be this way" moment of this new birth story. Then the crying began.

Not alone

March 2, 2003— I finally got this journal— it is to be an outlet for me during this postpartum time. Anastasia was born two months ago Tuesday, and I have spent the last few weeks going out of my mind. I began to wonder if it was more than "just me" after Shannon's mention of "keeping an eye on" this "depression thing," to make sure it's not something more. Pretty sure now it is PPD.

I've read the story of one woman who had it and saw a lot of myself in it. *Sleepless Days* by Susan Kushner Reswick really helped me through, knowing I'm not alone in my feelings. I wish I'd gotten this journal earlier, as I planned to write down some of her words that echoed my feelings. I found one passage that struck a chord. She writes about watching her baby, saying goodbye in her mind because she feels like she is leaving him. Filled with regret and apology, she is mourning the loss of herself and her family.[1]

I know the look of sorrow she gave her son, because I have given it to both of my kids. I am not the mother I once was to my first-born child, Jesse. He struggles to get and keep my attention. I struggle to give it to him. Why is this so darn hard?! I need to take a nap.

My heart aches for this younger version of myself, hurting and uncertain. "This is not forever," I want to tell her. "You will grow past this."

I realized I was no longer the mother I once was to my precious, active toddler. All I wanted to do was run away from home—go anywhere, it didn't matter—and never come back. I felt so sad about this, not the way a young mother is supposed to feel after having a new baby. It certainly wasn't the way I'd felt after Jesse was born. At that time, I was excited about my new role. The two of us went everywhere together; I even took him to a rummage sale when he was six days old! Looking back, I now know that was a little crazy, but I felt fine and wanted to get out and enjoy life. After Anastasia was born, I wanted to curl up into a big ball and disappear. What a radical difference.

From me to you

If you are feeling that something is not quite right, consider taking an online assessment for postpartum depression like my friend suggested to me. (I have included one in the Further Reading in the back of the book, but if the link is no longer active, a quick search of the internet can provide some results.) Get a notebook and write down how you are feeling. Be aware of mood swings you notice in yourself. It is essential to your family that you take care of your mental health as well as your baby.

Control

March 3— That nap yesterday was great— and even better was the night. I got my coveted four hours of sleep in a row! Praise God! And Anastasia slept for five hours, which is "sleeping through the night." Now to work on a feeding, wake time, nap/sleep schedule as we had with Jesse. Her gas still seems painful. I ordered a natural remedy as suggested by the nurse moms at the Look What I Can Do playgroup. Can't wait for that to come. The past three evenings, from 4-11, she had been fussy and nursing a lot. She didn't sleep much and always wanted to be held. Seems *much* better tonight! Again, praise God! Emotionally I have been okay. Not losing my temper or feeling sad or overwhelmed. Brent encouraged me to think positively the other day, and I am working on that. I also need to relinquish my need for control and admit that I am not, nor will I ever be, the perfect parent. But I am doing enough. I'm a loving mother, and I'm doing the best I can right now.

As a young mother, I was so optimistic about establishing a sleep and feeding schedule. This, I told myself, would provide the much-needed control over my chaotic life with a newborn and PPD. My son had been a relatively happy baby, aside from some gas pain he experienced, which was relieved by drops administered to him orally as needed. My daughter was his opposite in so many ways. When she started out so incredibly fussy, we thought it was just the same gassy experience. It was hard to imagine that this baby would not be the same as our first.

From me to you

If you have already had a child, resist the urge to compare their behaviors, especially if you are going through PPD. You will want to fight to maintain control and often end up disappointed when things do not go the way you think they should go. Does this mean you should not try to put your baby on a sleeping and feeding schedule? Absolutely not. However, please know it is not a magical cure for your PPD.

Are there things you are trying to control right now? Write them down. Consider if it's truly possible for you to change those situations.

Focus on the positive

March 4— I am struggling right now as the depression tries to make my situation seem worse than it really is. I was supposed to go to a meeting tonight and take a new sponsor with me. But it is snowing a lot and so she's not going, and because of the weather, we decided I shouldn't go either. I am more disappointed than I should be. I can't shake it. It's ridiculous to feel so disappointed over this. I also was supposed to get an award for my other sponsor. So that is a disappointment, too. But I should focus on the positive. Brent said he'd play a game with me tonight. So I am glad about that. Focus on the positive. I get to spend time with Brent. Thank you, God, for that. I think the hardest part of this PPD is that some days are great, some are blah, and some just suck. The emotions can just take over without notice.

Prior to my pregnancy, I had become a consultant for a home party business. It was a great way for me to get out of the house, to make some money, and to talk to other women. In this journal entry, I am reminded of the disappointment of canceled events due to circumstances beyond my control and the extreme mood swings associated with postpartum depression.

The hardest part of the PPD mood swings is that I had no idea an episode was coming. I couldn't see the change in me until I was in the midst of it. The day before this disappointment, I had written in the journal about a good day, with stable emotions. And then WHAM! I was in quicksand, struggling to keep my head above ground and not fully despair. It was an emotional roller coaster.

Depression lies. It tells you that things will never get better, that the bad will only get worse. It sucks you in, pulls you down, and smothers you. Knowing that helps, but it can still be difficult to see beyond its haze.

Disappointment and lack of control team up against you. My husband tried to help me stay positive. He tried to find ways to help me amidst the mess that was in my mind: the sadness, the hopelessness, the struggle.

From me to you

When you notice you have experienced a mood swing, write about it and how it makes you feel. What can you learn from it? What positive things can you focus on today? Write them down and think about them throughout your day and night. This is basic meditation, and, throughout this book, I will revisit using positive thinking as a tool to help you through the fog of depression.

Asking for help

March 6— Last night was so hard. Jesse was sick and he threw up— just as I was getting ready for bed. Then Ana started screaming. Needless to say, I think it was an hour or more before I finally got to bed. Anastasia wasn't ready to sleep, so Brent held her so I could get some sleep. Today was difficult. Jesse being sick did not help the fact that I was so sleepy and exhausted. Not sure if Brent's going to feed Ana tonight because he has to get up early to take his mom to the dentist for surgery. I asked for help from church last week, and Adele called back today to tell me she's working on it. I am really hoping that a person coming once a week to help me clean would be helpful to my PPD.

In all honesty, I do not remember this event, and I had forgotten about calling the church ministry for help. Even now, I can feel the despair that an event such as this would have caused in my mind: deep, difficult to see clearly past the moment. All I wanted to do was sleep and then my kid vomited on me. It was more than what my mom always referred to while I was growing up: "Murphy's Law: If anything can go wrong, it will." That could be laughed off, though. When your mind isn't clouded by depression, it's definitely easier to roll with life's punches. During depression, however, it is incredibly difficult to even see that the punches might ever end.

From me to you

One thing I did which would end up making a large impact on my life was that I asked for help. I will return to this topic again in the book, but for now, put the idea out of your mind that asking for help means you are helpless, weak, or needy. It simply means you accept that it's too hard to do things on your own at this time. In the throes of PPD, you may need reminding that this is just a season where you need to be willing to put aside your "I am strong and can handle this myself" mentality and be open to asking for and receiving help.

Do you have trouble asking for help? Consider why and write about it. What do you need most right now? Who could you ask for assistance today?

Breaking through the numbness

March 7— What a horrible night! Jesse was up more than half the night crying. Almost nothing soothed him. We tried sleeping with him in our bed, on the floor of his room, holding him in the rocker. Brent took a vapor bath with him and watched TV with him at 2:30 a.m., while I nursed Anastasia. Finally around 3:30 we decided to let him cry himself to sleep after giving him some Tylenol. We all fell asleep for a while. I think it was an hour later that he woke me up again. I held him for a little while then laid him back down again, still crying. At 6:30 a.m. he was crying again. I had Brent get him out of bed because I was nursing, and Jesse was still whiney. He fell asleep briefly on the floor next to Brent's side of the bed. Finally, I put him back in his crib. He seems to be asleep again. We were scheduled to go see the pediatrician for Ana's two-month checkup today anyway. I hope she has some answers! It was so heart-breaking, the way he cried and screamed and whined. Oh, what nightmares I had about it, too! God, please heal him or at least ease this pain— whatever it may be. Please take care of our little boy. Last night You allowed me to feel for him instead of being numb or apathetic. Our house is actually quiet now. I think I'll finish breakfast and try to get more sleep!

Feeling something beside anger or sadness was a positive for me at this point in the journey. My heart was reawakened as my sweet boy acted out of character. He was rarely this way; in fact, a good friend of mine jokingly referred to him as "angel baby" because of her contrastingly difficult child. Something had to be wrong with Jesse for him to act this way, and we would get to the doctor later that day, but actually *feeling* for him was something new in my PPD journey. Postpartum depression had made me want to be numb. It hurt too much to feel. I hated how angry I was, and I was ashamed of my desires to escape my family and my life. Yet here I was, in the early months of my PPD, desperate to feel again, and God provided a way, through the sickness of my little man.

From me to you

Where are you numb in your life right now? Where does it hurt to feel? Are you willing to allow yourself to experience painful emotions instead of staying in an emotional holding pattern? Consider these things and write about them.

Celebrate
small victories

March 8— Jesse has an ear infection. Poor little man. This bathtime has become some of my most cherished time since Anastasia's birth [written in the bathtub]. Though I always wonder if I'm going to have to rush out to feed her or take care of Jesse. Brent is with Jesse now, who is crying because of his ear infection. I should be getting Ana up in 20 minutes to eat. Hopefully she'll sleep till then. I'm trying to cut down on my chocolate eating, per the *Postpartum Survival Guide* suggestion [caffeine may lead to anger and anxiety].[2] But I only seem to be binging on it even more. I'm not crazy enough to try a diet right now. The book made it clear that it's not a good idea to start anything new that you might be able to put off. But I do want to eat better, as per its suggestion— also try exercising to get my endorphins going and give me energy. I haven't had a really bad day in a while. But I know it could be around the corner, so I try not to let my guard down. I make sure to voice my feelings to Brent and not just mope or wallow in them. I am more assertive in a healthy way now. Amen! I feel my resentment towards Anastasia slipping away. Hooray! She seems to be taking to this four-hour schedule very well. She's gaining weight fine. It also helps that she's smiling and interacting more. Also the gripe water I got to ease her gas pain seems to be doing the trick. Hooray!

I was a young mother, with only 20 months' experience, and I did not know what was wrong with my son. Would it have been obvious if I had not been in a PPD fog? I can't say, but I'm grateful that the doctor had an answer for me.

Celebrating the small victories was essential during those days of PPD. As I read and learned more about the illness, I sought to treat myself in a manner that would facilitate healing. I am grateful for the advice I got and the resources I found. Together, they helped make this struggle more manageable. Also, as a new mother, it's so easy to forget that you have your own needs when there is a tiny person demanding all of you, especially when you are nursing. I struggled for self-care time. I found some relief in taking hot baths. Often my husband spent time with our toddler, so I could relax in a bubble bath with my journal.

I also started reading and working my way through a devotional book on depression, recommended by two friends who had prior experience with it. The book, co-written by a pastor and a physician, was *Conquering Depression: A Thirty-Day Plan to Finding Happiness* (see Further Reading for more information). It proved instrumental in my healing over the following months. I highly recommend this book for anyone going through any type of depression.

In my journal I interacted with some of the truths from the book, such as these:

- God is more powerful than my depression.
- God's love for me will help me win against depression.
- I will continue to believe that God loves me despite my feelings.[3]

From me to you

What can you celebrate today? Did you hold your tongue when you felt like yelling? Did you get out of bed? Did you go outside? All of these things are worth celebrating while you are going through PPD. Look at the list of truths mentioned above. What are your responses to those statements? Take some time to write them in your journal.

Finding comfort

March 9— Last night I spent a lot of time holding Anastasia because she was so fussy and had gas again, the first really bad episode in a week. I bought my own copies of the PPD books [I had been using ones from the library], as well as *Meditations for Mothers of Toddlers* and *Meditations for New Mothers* both by Beth Wilson Saavedra. The author asserted the need for a mother to have time alone as a way to prepare her for the time spent with her child.[4] What a necessary reminder of my need for alone time. I plan to write that on a note card and put it on the wall here by my rocker chair. I actually did one productive thing before diagnosing my PPD— I created this reading corner in my bedroom. I am just starting to enjoy it. Jesse slept through last night! Praise God! Ana, once she finally settled down enough that I could put her in bed without her screaming, slept about five hours. Hooray!

In my attempts to diagnose myself (since we were between insurance policies and my husband wanted me to wait so we wouldn't have a "pre-existing condition"), I read every book on postpartum depression I could find. The books served as a comfort, a voice of reason, a "friend" who had been where I was. Setting aside time for reading and quiet was essential to my well being during those early days. I sought help and learned from others' experiences and stories. Writing about it in my journal helped me to get through each day and see the progress I was making.

From me to you

Take whatever time you are able to find and seek quiet on your own. It may be five minutes in the bathroom (even if you don't have to use the toilet!) or on the back porch in a patio chair. Try putting a devotional in the bathroom so you are able to redeem that time. Consider making a basket of books, with a journal and a pen, and put it by the front door to pick up as you leave the house for time alone, or make a reading corner in your house as I did.

Confidence beyond circumstances

March 9 (later)— In the financial shape we are in, the strain Ana has put on us is more than I can understand. Two weeks ago I asked why God allowed me to get pregnant at this time. But I know He has a plan bigger than our circumstances. He has given Brent peace during this time, making Brent more of a rock for our family. But I still struggle amidst all this. But God can provide me a peace, like Brent's, that transcends all understanding. "And the peace of God, which transcends all understanding, will guard your hearts and your minds in Christ Jesus." (Philippians 4:7) Thank God for the story of Elijah's depression. It makes things so much easier for the rest of us as we struggle. Thank You for the friends who have saddled up alongside me during this difficult time.

Also in my journal, I reflected more on the lessons I learned while reading the *Conquering Depression* book, studying Elijah's story. I recognized the despair the prophet felt as he fled from Jezebel's threats to take his life (I Kings 19). Often emotions narrow our focus, and we cannot see what is beyond the things we are feeling. I found myself stuck there, looking through eyes of hopelessness instead of faith.

From me to you

What difficult circumstances are you facing today? Trust can be defined as belief in the reliability or strength of someone or something. Do you find it easy or difficult to trust beyond what you can see? Take a few minutes to write about trust. Consider who or what you can trust to help you through this tough time.

The snowball effect

March 10— Well, I spoke too soon about Anastasia's gas. Soon as I wrote that in here, she had a couple of painful gas episodes. It's not as much as it used to be, but it's still a lot of pain and screaming when it does occur.

I am sooo MAD right now! I am letting little things snowball into a rage, and this journal is my outlet for them!!! Jesse is misbehaving— disobeying me, ignoring me, purposely stepping on Ana's hand. Then the baby gate fell down on my head and that hurt. Brent didn't put his dish in the dishwasher which annoyed me. He knows the ant problems we've been having! But he's sick (he got Jesse's cold). I'm fighting it myself. Anastasia is the only good thing right now. That's ironic since all that has happened in the past two months since her birth has driven me crazy. But she doesn't know. She's next to me on the bed, smiling and cooing, trying to grow up so I will pay more attention to her. I feel so forced sometimes when I'm with her. I did not want this pregnancy. It interrupted my weight loss efforts. It made me gain weight again. I allowed it to ruin my good eating habits. It caused us so much financial hardship. It has put immeasurable stress on my marriage and my relationship with Brent. But then I look at her and am ashamed. How can I feel that way, so resentful? I wouldn't trade her for any of it, I say. But somehow I wish I could have both worlds— with her and before her. I desperately want the "me" before she was born— the happy person, the skinnier, healthier person. I know I can have those things back. It will just take time. But I am very impatient! I want to be mentally well. I am struggling so much with this PPD. Though I know there are those who have it much worse. Am I putting too great of expectations on myself? I'm sure I am. How can I stop that? It is self-destructive.

One of the things that depression does is make it difficult to see what is really going on in a situation. As I reflect on this journal entry, I can see the thought spiral, the blaming, and the irrational thoughts, but I am powerless to stop them. I wish I could go back to myself and tell myself to take some deep breaths, focus on what is truly important, and release the negative.

From me to you

If you are experiencing these feelings, a counselor can help you work through them. One thing is certain, allowing little things to add up and make one big angry blow-up is not good for anyone. Writing them down can help you release them in a safe environment and keep you from an emotional explosion.

All new parents struggle. They need to learn to communicate better, to place each other's needs as priority, and to love well. Communication is so important. It is important to talk through our feelings and the situation. If you want to make sure you respond rather than react, take some time to write down what you want to say and then talk about it at a later time. Just try to catch it before it snowballs into an angry outburst.

No record of wrongs

March 10 (continued)— I am sooo MAD again. I feel like we're slipping back to the way things were before we talked a couple of weeks ago. Brent isn't spending time with me, and he isn't taking care of the kids. When he does, it seems he complains. Yes, he's sick. But am I wrong to think that if he's well enough to play poker on the computer all day and night, he's well enough to spend some time with me?!! Again he's postponed our date, saying he doesn't feel up to it. But last night he went to bed early instead of the date. Tonight he's on the computer. I AM SO MAD!! I had to put Jesse to bed myself (usually his responsibility). I feel like I'm doing everything and that it's always going to be this way. I <u>know</u> these thoughts and feelings are irrational. But I don't care. I just want to <u>YELL!!</u> I know that my emotions are just out of control. It's weird— I was getting more and more upset and had a desperate need to get to my journal and write. I was afraid

I'd **BURST** if I didn't. Anastasia seems to be resisting the schedule I want to put her on, which is also frustrating. But whatever— she will eventually get on one. I just need to keep trying.

Writing about how I felt, instead of angrily confronting my husband in instances like this, is what saved our relationship. It's important to clarify the difference between journaling these feelings and confiding in a friend. Despite how you are feeling in the midst of PPD, you certainly *do not* want to destroy your marriage. Telling a friend about every negative thought you have about your husband is not productive; it is dishonoring to your husband and your marriage partnership. It can also lead to gossip and lack of trust between spouses. Without a doubt, when clear thinking comes after the emotions have passed, a wife will most certainly regret dragging her husband's name through the mud.

Reviewing my journal helped me see changes I wanted to make in the way I reacted to my husband. I found I was glad I wrote it down instead, so that I could go back to it a few days later, when I was in a clear frame of mind and see if it was really worth getting upset over. Sometimes it was something worth confronting my husband about, but more often, I decided to forebear and move on.

From me to you

In I Corinthians 13, Paul writes about love: what it is and what it is not. One truth that sticks out to me is in verse five: "It does not dishonor others, it is not self-seeking, it is not easily angered, it keeps no record of wrongs." If you are angry about something, take some time to journal. When you have written down all that you are angry about, see which ones you can release. Think of them no more. This will do wonders for your relationship and help your mood, too.

More to my Life

March 10 (continued)—Sometimes I feel as if my life is a never-ending load of laundry or dishes. Housework seems to consume my "free time" (time when kids are asleep). It's so frustrating!

I just watched the movie *Life or Something Like It*. The main character is told by a street "prophet" that she is going to die in a week. By the end of the movie, she has learned how to live each day as if it is her last. What would I change about my life to live to the fullest? I thought right away that I'd spend more time with Jesse: playing, reading, doing things with him. Right now I'm in a holding pattern with him. I "maintain" him by taking care of his immediate physical needs, but I neglect the more important needs to interact with him. Lord, show me ways to be purposeful with him each day, starting tomorrow. Help me to build a spiritual foundation, a basis upon which he will grow. Help me to <u>play</u> with him. And this goes for Anastasia too. I am having such a difficult time balancing their needs and their play, too.

Maintaining balance is hard for all people. We typically feel pulled in so many different directions and struggle to keep priorities where they belong. As a young mother experiencing PPD and in survival mode, I did not even consider what my priorities should be. It's now evident to me that I was a shell of the mother I had been before PPD invaded my life. My attempts to talk to myself about living life to its fullest meant engaging in my children's lives, rather than just doing the minimum. Writing the words was a start, but it would be a long struggle to get to that place without it feeling forced.

From me to you

What priorities have you let slide? Where do you want to make changes in your life? Take one step at a time toward the change you want to make regarding balance and priorities. It will not happen overnight, but it will happen if it is important to you.

Feeling desperate

March 14— Today Brent saw how truly desperate I am with this PPD. I had an irritating morning phone call to Sylvia in which I was seeking advice on how to get rid of the ants in my carpet and loveseat. She told me I had two choices: to tell Brent to get his butt out of bed and help me clean (to get rid of the ants) or leave him a note asking for a divorce, take the kids, and go to my parents' house. After that, I got off the phone. Jesse, Ana, and Brent were all upstairs, and I was downstairs. I let out the loudest, angriest yell I can remember. I said to God, "I can't do this alone." I kicked the couch. Brent wanted to make sure I was okay, so he yelled down to ask. I told him through sobs that it was just what I needed to do right now and proceeded to yell out again and sob loudly as I walked around the living room and kitchen of our tiny townhome. After it was quiet, Brent asked if it was safe to bring Jesse down. He came down with Jesse (who was probably confused by my screaming). Brent held me and asked what was going on. I told him what was said to me. A little while later, we talked about it some more. He said that he heard "anguish" in my screams. I explained that was how I was feeling. He wanted to fix it, and I told him he couldn't. I need to see a therapist, but I have to wait until we get a new insurance policy. God, help me to make it through.

I am trying some of the coping strategies in the survival guide, one being cutting down on chocolate consumption. I am limiting myself to three pieces a day. Brent is holding me accountable. Limiting chocolate consumption should help with the anxiety and anger I am experiencing. How I pray that this step is in the right direction. I am also trying to add fruit and veggies to my diet again. I'm trying to be more thoughtful in meal preparation. Yesterday was a busy errands day, and I coped okay. The day before I took a walk with the kids and got some frustration out that way. It was Fiona's great idea! Baths are good, too. This one is especially hot and I am sweating. Feels good. I missed this when I was pregnant.

My heart literally aches for the younger me in this situation. I want to hug her and assure her that she will get through this, that she will not always feel this way. Also, I would tell her that one person's snarky comment does not have to ruin her day. Though depression makes it harder to respond to negative comments or suggestions, try not to give them a prominent place in your mind.

Physical health is important when dealing with depression. Diet can affect a person's mood. But, as shown above, I clung to the hope that it would help more than it possibly could. Emotional eating was a struggle, and since I didn't drink coffee or tea, chocolate and soft drinks were my two sources of caffeine.

From me to you

Has someone said something unkind to you, even hurtful? Consider writing it down. Look for truth in it. If there is nothing good you can learn from it, release it and move on. When you feel like there's nothing else you can do, take a step in the right direction. Then take one more. Every effort helps on the road to healing.

Thoughts and grief

March 19— This past week has been interesting, as I struggled with going overboard on chocolate Monday and Sunday. Today I haven't had any at all— and I don't want any. I avoided caffeine at the mall for lunch. I want to do what I can to beat PPD. My parents were here yesterday and today. It was so good to spend time with them, and it was great for Jesse to see them. I wish they didn't live so far away.

I was just reading *This Isn't What I Expected: Overcoming Postpartum Depression* by Karen Kleiman and Valerie Davis Raskin. I was overwhelmed by the power negative thinking can play in PPD for me. Admitting out loud "I have postpartum depression" and "This is not my fault" was helpful. I cried as I said it over and over. Here are the other positive affirmations I could say:

- I am going through postpartum depression. These are real symptoms of a real illness.
- I can receive treatment and get better.
- Though things don't look good at the moment, I will not always hurt.
- I am not losing my mind.
- Nothing I did caused this to happen in my life.
- Some days will be good, and others will be bad, but I won't always feel this way.
- Choices I make will help me feel better.[5]

Thoughts can turn a mood dark or light. They can lift us up or pull us down. Reading those affirmations was a turning point for me. I continued to read and learned that the typical pattern of recovery for PPD included five steps: using what I have to pull myself out; seeking professional help if needed, asking those around me to help, taking time to grieve the losses I've experienced since the birth, and being able to look past the illness to a clear future.[6] Reading those steps gave me a plan, and it pleased the list-maker in me to have steps towards healing I could accomplish. It gave me a goal.

From me to you

Make sure to allow yourself time to grieve any losses you may have experienced since the birth of your child. You have lost the freedom to "get up and go" on a moment's notice. You may have lost closeness in your relationship with your husband. Your relationship with your other children may be strained. You haven't slept much. Your friendships may have changed as you became a parent and other friends did not. Some people don't know how to handle your gloomy mood, so they seem to avoid you. You don't have the idealized, fantasy scenario—whatever that may have meant for you. Your child will not follow the expert-recommended schedule, and you seemingly have no time for yourself. It is healthy to grieve those losses. It helps you to move on. It may help you to take some time and journal about them.

The power of love

March 19 (continued)— Sunday in church, God used the pastor's message to speak to my heart about how much He loves me. It's more than I can understand, but I can seek God to get a handle on it. And then we sang a response song which I felt was written just for me. It was "Hungry (Falling on My Knees)" written by Kathryn Scott. Each word spoke to me and God's love washed over me.

During my depression, my church presented a four-week series called "The Power of Love." It was all about God's love. I got myself copies of the sermons on cassette— yes, it was that long ago!— and listened to them over and over again. I allowed the truths in the messages to combat the negative thoughts: the anger, the bitterness, the resentment, the loneliness, the hurt, the hopelessness, and the depression.

From me to you

Depression's trick is to make you believe you are not worthy of love. As a result, you may be filled with shame. Then, the downward spiral of your feelings mixes with the negative thoughts you tell yourself, and it pulls you deeper into a pit, one that you are unable to climb out of no matter what you do.

But I want to tell you these truths:

- You are loved by the God who created the universe. (See Romans 8:39 and Ephesians 2:4)
- You are more precious to Him than you can fathom. (See Psalm 139.)
- He sent His Son to die, so that you may live. (See John 3:16 and Romans 5:8.)

Live in light of these truths. Let them set you free. Bask in the glow of the love of Christ. Seek Him daily and ask Him to reveal His love to you. He will.

Meditate on this prayer, written by Paul, in his letter to the church at Ephesus: "I pray that out of His glorious riches He may strengthen you with power through His Spirit in your inner being, so that Christ may dwell in your hearts through faith. And I pray that you, being rooted and established in love, may have power, together with all the Lord's holy people, to grasp how wide and long and high and deep is the love of Christ, and to know this love that surpasses knowledge— that you may be filled to the measure of all the fullness of God." (Ephesians 3:16-19)

Longing for more

March 19 (continued)— I desperately long to be close to God again, close to my husband again, too. I long not to be depressed, angry, bitter, resentful, lonely, hurting, hopeless— all these feelings I struggle with. God, help me!

Many times I found myself surrounded by people yet feeling completely alone. Even God felt far away. One essential way to combat those feelings— because that's all they were, not truths— was to be intentional about spending time in prayer daily with God.

Seeking God during this time of PPD was instrumental for my working through the haze. It didn't bring me the "cure" that so many people think will happen. This illness could not be wished away, but I could take positive steps in my relationships to bring me towards healing. Going to church and participating in times of corporate worship were two choices I made to help myself on the road to recovery.

From me to you

Do you long for more? Are you feeling alone? Does God feel far away? Try to read at least one scripture verse a day to draw closer to Him. Don't buy Satan's lie: You are <u>not</u> alone. Take a minute to pray now— silently, out loud, or written in your journal. Consider attending church services. If you do not have a church home, ask a friend where she attends and join her. If you don't know anyone who goes to church, try an internet search for congregations in your area. Often you are able to view a portion of the service online before you attend to help you see if it's the right place for you. Being surrounded by others as you seek God may be a comfort in your depression.

Knowledge empowers

March 20— It's so good to know that many of my physical issues are symptoms of PPD— sugar and carb cravings, overeating, excessive sleeping, headaches, lack of energy, poor concentration, and more. Then there are the emotional symptoms! I feel as if I could identify with 90 percent of them listed on page 45 of *This Isn't What I was Expecting*: inadequacy, sadness, guilt, isolation, anger, resentment, shame, loss of control, lack of confidence, scary fantasies (running away from home is my big one), feeling not myself, being overwhelmed, poor concentration, excessive crying, loneliness, helplessness, anxiety, fear, hopelessness, irritability, low self-esteem, oversensitivity, and extreme agitation.[7] Today I made up a song to the tune of one of Jesse's VeggieTales songs. "God is bigger than my depression. He's bigger than my sadness and the anger that I feel. He's going to deliver me from these blues."

Learning more about PPD was extremely encouraging. It helped remind me that I was not alone, that it was not my fault, and that I could get through it. Recognizing that truth and seeing myself in the symptoms listed in a book empowered me.

Being the mother of a toddler as well as a newborn meant watching lots of children's videos to make it through the day. One favorite was VeggieTales. I found myself identifying with Junior Asparagus, a young veggie who was frightened by a movie he watched before bedtime. To comfort him, Bob and Larry sing him a song called "God is Bigger" in the episode "Where's God When I'm S-Scared." I found that making up my own lyrics was a positive affirmation I could hold onto during a tough day.

From me to you

What physical symptoms of PPD are you experiencing? Which emotional ones can you identify with from my list above? Find a book about PPD at the library (the ones I read are listed in Further Reading), order a copy from your online bookstore, or take part of your day to visit a local bookstore and purchase one there. I believe you will find that knowledge is a powerful step toward your healing.

Household help

March 21— I am so grateful. God brought a woman from my church into my life who has had PPD. She volunteered as part of Heartlight (church ministry) to help clean my house. We got talking and she told me upfront about her experience. Her name is Miranda. She went to the PPD support group I am considering and recommends it. She also wants to get together sometime. Thank you, God!! I'm having a chocolate day. I just crave it so much— I gave in. Oh well, since I can't take a nap today, I am indulging. I am taking a bubble bath now.

The church I attended at the time had a ministry called Heartlight, which helped people meet a variety of needs through service, such as visiting shut-ins and cooking meals for new mothers. The ministry leader asked me what they could do to help me. I desperately asked for help cleaning my house because I just couldn't handle that part of life.

From me to you

Does the thought of doing laundry overwhelm you right now? How do you feel about cleaning the kitchen? Perhaps you can receive help from a trusted source. Ask a friend, a family member, or your church for assistance in completing these tasks.

Confront and feel emotions

March 21 (continued)—

- I will allow myself to feel extreme agitation.
- I will allow myself to feel anger.
- I will allow myself to feel sugar/starch cravings.
- I will allow myself to feel my lack of energy.
- I will allow myself to feel sadness.
- I will allow myself to feel resentment.
- I will allow myself to feel guilt.
- I will allow myself to feel helplessness.
- I will allow myself to feel irritability.
- I will allow myself to feel overwhelmed.

As I went through them, reading them aloud, it was so apparent which ones I'd been trying to deny or pretend didn't exist— the cravings, the lack of energy, the sadness, being overwhelmed. I guess I thought (wrongly) that if I didn't think about them, I could get over them.

This was an exercise in the book *This Isn't What I Expected*. It suggested I list the physical and emotional symptoms that were most troublesome to me at the present. After I listed some of them, the authors encouraged me to confront the feelings and give myself permission to have them. This was designed to help me reduce my resistance to the emotions I was experiencing.

I learned that it was important to accept the feelings and respect them, not to fight them or be afraid of them. It turned out that not fighting them was the most difficult for me. I mistakenly thought that if I was strong enough or used enough positive thinking techniques, by my will I could make the feelings go away, possibly because I grew up in a home where I was discouraged from showing emotion. By resisting the feelings or questioning them, I gave them power to harm me. I needed to learn to release the power they had over me.

Though I wrote those words 19 years ago, the lesson tucked into the back of my brain. I now recall the many times over the years I have encouraged my kids to name what was bothering them, be it in a dream or how they were feeling, to reduce the power it had over them. I did not remember that this exercise had its genesis back in my PPD days.

From me to you

Do you allow yourself to *feel* the emotions, or do you try to suppress them? Try the exercise as I did above. Admitting the truth about your situation to yourself can really help set you free. As Jesus told His disciples in John 8:32, "You will know the truth, and the truth will set you free."

Good and bad days

March 23— I'm having a hard day and I'm not sure why. I guess that's just part of PPD. I'm not going to question "why" but "what can I do" instead. So what can I do today? I can remember all that I learned at church this morning about God's love for me <u>NOT</u> being performance-based.

It's part of His character, who He is. It has nothing to do with my actual <u>being</u>, except that I simply BE. I am His creation so He loves me. A worship song spoke to my heart this morning: "My Heart Will Trust" by Darlene Zschech and Hillsong. Amen!

There will be good days and bad days in the journey of PPD. Finding the positive things or learning what helps to turn one's mood is a key to making it through a low day.

From me to you

Talk to yourself, out loud if you must. Speak truth and affirmations, sing songs— do whatever it takes to help you through a bad day. Consider which songs speak truth to your heart and make a playlist. Listen to it often.

Shared experience

March 24— A good morning today. A rough afternoon/evening. Getting out of the house really helps me, I think. When I feel trapped by Ana's feeding schedule or Jesse's nap schedule or the idea of running an errand with the two of them, I feel overwhelmed, suffocated. I need to be able to just assert my needs to Brent and give her a bottle and pump later, I guess. I need to place the demands on him for help when I feel this way. It worked— Brent agreed to what I told him I wanted for tomorrow morning.

I talked with Adele today. She'll be coming over Wednesday to help me for an hour. She also suffered from PPD, but she had a thyroid dysfunction. Mine probably isn't that. I pray our insurance comes through soon.

I gorged myself on chocolate and sweets today, and I feel terrible about it. I just finished reading the section in *This Isn't What I Expected* about exercise and its benefits for depression. Endorphins evoke feelings of well being (antidepressant). I want to try tomorrow morning.

The knowledge that others had experienced what I was feeling and survived was so comforting. I am beyond grateful for each and every woman who opened up to me about her struggle.

From me to you

Who do you know who has experienced depression? Ask friends if they know anyone. Perhaps your church staff or a local moms' group can help you connect with someone. If you are able to find other women who have gone through PPD and are willing to sit and talk or just listen, it's worth your time. It can become the lighthouse beacon to keep you from crashing into the rocks during the deep fog of your depression. See Further Reading in the back of the book for resources to connect to local PPD support groups.

Visual reminder

March 25— I feel so great! I did my workout video for 15 minutes this morning. Hooray! I figured that was a good start, and I'd heard Anastasia crying. Brent got her to fall back asleep, so I got to take a nice hot shower, too!

I decided to make a calendar to record these things: worked out, limited chocolate, great days, good days, quiet time, got out of the house, and whatever other things come up along the way which are positive towards my recovery.

A no-chocolate day! Hooray!

Anastasia is so smiley right now. She's cooing and kicking, and it's so great. I had about an hour or so tonight when I was upset and depressed. It hit me out of nowhere like a sledgehammer. But somehow I got out of it. I was having thoughts of gorging myself on chocolate, but instead had a PopTart and a banana. I want to start eating better, but I'm taking it one step at a time, especially regarding chocolate. Hope to get up again tomorrow morning and work out.

I am a visual learner, and that's why I decided to make a calendar to record the following good things: work-out out, limited chocolate, great days (no depressed feelings), good days (not many depressed feelings), quiet time with God (Bible study and/or prayer), got out of the house, and other things that I experienced that were positive towards my recovery.

For many years, I held onto that calendar on my bookshelf, alongside my journals and books on post-partum depression. I kept it as a sign that days pass, and some are not good, but when they're all put together, the good often outweighs the bad.

It was easy to see some patterns and reactions to changes in my behavior over time. I noticed that days when I worked out were generally better days for me, as seen on my calendar, which also helped me to see what other things were good for me—adult interaction, limiting chocolate, eating fruit, and getting out of the house. Though I no longer have this calendar, I remember writing on it and being able to look and see the progress, especially later in my PPD.

From me to you

Could a calendar like I described be helpful to you? Set attainable goals or just list things you want to see happen, and then keep track of it in some way (calendar, chart, journal, etc.). Success in any of the areas where you are currently struggling can be a huge boost for your depressed mood.

Accepting assistance

March 26— Too tired this morning— chose sleep instead of working out. Adele from church came over and did some cleaning for me this morning. We talked too. She is going to try to get us help from church for our other needs (diapers, etc.).

Some people allow their pride to get in the way and won't accept help when they need it. Of my many struggles, that has never been one of them. The way I see it, people gain so much when they help others, so how could I deny them the satisfaction that comes from being a blessing? What a blessing these women were to me. Many of them I did not know prior to asking for help, but their hearts of service brought them to me through the ministry.

From me to you

Believe it or not, there are people out there who *want* to help you with the things you just can't do in this season of your life, such as the dishes. Seriously. Yes, it means humbling yourself and asking for help or simply responding to an offer someone makes. Vocalize your practical needs and allow them to help you. This is their spiritual act of worship; allow them the pleasure and help yourself at the same time. The Apostle Peter wrote, "Each of you should use whatever gift you have received to serve others, as faithful stewards of God's grace in its various forms." (I Peter 4:10)

If your church does not have such a ministry, ask someone at the church office to refer you to someone who would want to help you, or ask friends, family, or neighbors. If you can afford it and don't have a church you attend, hire help. But don't underestimate how much allowing someone to help you blesses her, too. As Paul wrote in Philippians 2:4 (NLT), "Don't look out only for your own interests, but take an interest in others, too."

Managing anger

March 26 (continued)— I know I need to stop focusing on Brent and his shortcomings at this time when I'm having a hard enough time myself. I had him put Jesse's dirty diaper in the Genie [a special garbage can for diapers to keep the smell from overwhelming the room]. Then he came back and said, "Just so you know, the Genie's full." That comment made me upset because he never wants to learn how to take care of that, and I started crying. I think it would have been more, but Jesse's here next to me in the tub and I don't want to upset him. I suddenly feel empty, like a shell of myself. I can look down and see my pathetic self and wonder how I got here. Who is this person who is living my life? Where did I go? Will I ever come back? I feel hopelessness. And I will allow myself to feel hopelessness. It is a symptom of my PPD. I will not feel this way forever.

Sometimes I just want to quit. It's so hard being a mom. I'm so tired. When Jesse acts like he did earlier, I just have to grit my teeth and hold myself back. I want to hit him. [However, I did not.] I don't remember feeling this way before Ana's birth, so I guess it must be a symptom of my PPD.

If I could go back and talk to myself on that day, I would assure this hopeless mother that it was going to be okay. She would eventually get through it. The loss of control over a situation which led to anger and thoughts about wanting to strike my child was indeed a symptom of PPD, feelings which I would continue to deal with for the next decade. It would not be until then that I fully understood the reasons behind my anger with my children and how I could learn to release it in nonviolent, non-threatening ways instead of allowing it to build up and result in verbal outbursts.

From me to you

Do you feel anger more intensely as a result of your PPD? Acknowledge your emotions. Write about your anger and avoid taking it out on those around you. If you continue to struggle with anger as a mom, I have some resources to recommend, once you've made it through the PPD fog. See Further Reading at the end of this book.

Get out!

March 31— It's been a few days since I've written what I've experienced. Some bad days. Shannon is moving this week, which makes me sad. She has been so helpful through this time.

I've been able to see some patterns and reactions to changes in my behavior. Days when I work out are generally better days for me. The calendar is helping me to see what other things are good— adult interaction, limiting chocolate, eating fruit, getting out of the house.

I met Lily from church, a woman who spoke on conquering depression at church last year. She had PPD, too. She highly recommended the book Fiona loaned me. She suggested that I need to get out of the house regularly away from the kids— by myself to do something for myself. Brent seems supportive. I plan to ask friends to watch the kids for an hour so I can do that. Fiona has already said okay— looks like the second Tuesday of the month. Ideas I had for what I can do: go to the library and read for fun— fiction!, see a movie, eat a meal, workout, get a manicure and pedicure, get a makeover from Ally from church, work on scrapbooks, window shop— no errands or work. Anyway, Lily took the time to pray with me. I am so grateful for her.

I found that being outside in the nice weather of spring was helpful to me. There were also times I just needed to leave the house after being cooped up in it all day with the kids, despite the weather. I spent a lot of time at the library. Having supportive friends who made a way for me to have time on my own was a blessing, too!

From me to you

Find those people who will support you during this difficult time, those who will encourage and pull you along because they understand. Accept their help as the gift it is meant to be for you. Beware of isolation during this time. It's your worst enemy during this time, and getting out of the house can add to your healing. It helps you to see the world beyond the overwhelming motherhood mess. When you get out of the house, do something just for you. It does not have to cost much (or any) money. Sitting at a park and writing in a journal, taking a walk at a forest preserve, reading in a corner booth at the coffee shop, skipping stones at the beach, pulling out colored pencils and an adult coloring book at the library, grabbing a crochet hook and some yarn to make a small blanket in your backyard: choose what appeals to you and do it.

Seek support

April 1— I called and left the psychiatrist a message regarding the DAD (Depression after Delivery) group. My insurance will hopefully be in effect soon. Today wasn't bad, but I definitely didn't feel like myself. I felt kind of funky. Didn't get to work out, but we got to Mom & Me at Eva's house (church playgroup) and we went to the park, so I spent some time outside. It was gorgeous today— over 70°F! [I live in Illinois, so that is heavenly in April.] Anastasia was up a couple of times last night, so I didn't get much sleep in a row, which made me exhausted. But I got in a kind-of nap this afternoon— with Ana next to me because she wouldn't sleep without nursing. Having the two kids in the same bedroom isn't working so great yet. I need to find a solution. Brent and I are supposed to watch a movie together tonight, so that will give me a little more adult interaction. I did not have much time to talk with the other moms at Mom & Me today.

This Isn't What I Expected says to write out my needs, such as intimacy, reassurance, practical help, and advice, and list someone who can help meet them. I don't know who can help with advice. I am hoping a therapist could help. I turn to my books a lot and sometimes Jamie for childcare advice. Lily might give me PPD advice, now that I've met her. The nurses at Look What I Can Do playgroup are people I've turned to for advice.

While I deal with PPD, I need to watch out for isolation. It's dangerous. The book says I should make getting out of my house daily a priority in my life.[8] I have been working on this and have succeeded. Though I find it very helpful to have time outside as well. The weather has been nice, but it's going to get cold again this weekend, they say. Tomorrow night Brent is going out to play poker. I think I need to be mentally prepared for an evening alone with my kids, the first in a while.

Looking back on this, I am proud of this young mother who continued to try ideas from the book, to seek solutions to help her improve her mood with the resources she had available to her. I took the time and wrote down who could help me to meet my various needs, big or small.

From me to you

Who do you have who can help you meet your various needs? Are you willing to ask for that help? It may be helpful to list it out. Then when you are feeling alone in your situation, you can remember that *you are not alone*, and that these people *want* to help you. Knowing steps to take and then actually taking them can lead to successes, big and small. Celebrate them. Use them as a foundation toward your improved mental health. Reflect on them and learn from them.

Extrovert or introvert?

April 3— Yesterday was a good day, except for my cold I caught from Anastasia and the little sunburn I got on my face from being out at the park. [I am fair-skinned and sunburn easily.] After a morning at the park with Cara, I had an afternoon with Cathy. We painted wooden wall knob hangers for the kids' bedroom. Then Fiona came over, and it was all of us for dinner and talking. Then just me and Fiona (and the kids, of course). Jesse went to bed early, and once I got Ana down after they left, I was able to do a little paperwork (for my home party business) and get to bed by 10 p.m. But I was up at 12, 2, 3ish (Ana), and 5 (Ana). My throat is so sore; my nose hurts from sunburn and blowing it. My shoulders and back are tight; my whole body aches. So I'm enjoying a bath now. I've decided that I feel too miserable to attempt going to the playgroup, which makes me sad, because I really want to go. So I probably won't be at church tonight either. I have a home party event tomorrow night that I'd like to feel better for. Then a day and night alone with the kids on Saturday. Brent has a seminar in Milwaukee. I'll have to plan something to do, to go out and avoid depression.

Introvert and extrovert are personality types. Introverts tend to be reserved, enjoying most of their time alone or at home. Extroverts, on the other hand, are typically outgoing and tend to seek out social interaction. It's easy to see that I am an extrovert from all of the things I did with different people on this one day. Typically, I feel energized by being around people whereas, for some introverts, being around people drains them, especially if it is for a long period of time.

My daughter was born in early January, a time of year when people in Chicagoland are bundled up against the winter winds. People stay home in cold winter weather. There are not as many opportunities to be social in January and February. In contrast, my son was born in early June, so I was out and about within a week, visiting rummage sales, art festivals, and the zoo. The year he was born, I had eight friends from church who all had their babies within a month of each other, including my son! We always had someone to spend time with, somewhere to go, something to do.

From me to you

Putting aside feelings resulting from your PPD, would you typically consider yourself an introvert or an extrovert? How can you meet your need to be around others or your need to be alone? Do what works for you, but if you are experiencing depression, everything I read encourages getting out and interacting with others. If you are an introvert, you may need less of it, but remember your need to connect with people or just leave the house. Give permission to a trusted friend or your spouse to help you get out occasionally.

Communication is Key

April 3 (continued)— I am so upset with Brent and the breakdown of communication and understanding between us. I know half of it is on my end, but I wish he would just understand my needs. I <u>needed</u> to leave the house after being cooped up in it all day. He couldn't see that, because it's cold and rainy and I'm sick. He didn't think it was "wise." I told him I needed to do it for my emotional health. He doesn't seem to understand that I work 12- to 15-hour days with the kids, seven days a week. When I get a break, it's to go to my other job (home party shows) or run errands without kids. I can't remember the last time I did something just for me— without a kid or without Brent. Our communication issues need to be resolved. I don't want to ask for permission to leave the house. He pointed out that he asks permission for things, too. I see a really bad pattern in this. I'm not sure it's healthy.

I finally got a call back on the DAD support group. Jamie said she'd watch Jesse. I can't wait to go. I explained to the doctor my situation with insurance. She understood completely and was very supportive of my attending the group, which is free and does not require insurance. So anyway, I'm at the library now. I have an hour to myself. No screaming kids, no demands from anyone for attention— just me. Ahhhhh... So nice to be away. I know I need some more help than I have now with handling this PPD. But I am doing the best I can right now. I have a feeling that the library may become my refuge in this PPD. I so desperately want to feel like myself again! I want to lose the weight I gained and feel as good as I did a year ago. I don't want to have any more kids. I don't want to do this again. I want <u>me</u> back!

In marriage, communication is essential, and when I was experiencing PPD, I spent a lot of time writing in my journal, debating over what to say to my husband and when. Depression can cloud a lot of what is actually happening and cause confusion. It can make us lose sight of what is really happening. Time runs more slowly. It was just a few days earlier that I realized the importance of leaving the house for "me" time, yet the way I wrote above makes it seem like ages.

In *This Isn't What I Expected*, the authors titled a chapter "Helping Your Husband Help You." I journaled through some of the communication issues listed, including not assuming my husband knows how I am feeling and avoiding being vague. I realized I needed to ask for practical help and specify my needs. Whether or not my husband chooses to help is up to him, but he might not know what needs to be done unless I ask.

Our marriage has had its ups and downs. We were married six and a half years before the birth of our second child, but nothing could have prepared us for such a difficult time with my PPD. To top it off, my husband was in a commission-only sales job which was very unsteady, so we had financial pressures added to the mix.

Things that may have bothered me before PPD now infuriated me. I wanted him to change the way he had been our entire marriage, possibly because I couldn't control anything else. However, I did not take the time to communicate my feelings, which put a strain on our marriage. In my journal I wondered, "Are my expectations unreasonable? I don't know. Maybe we need marital counseling. I know I need to stop focusing on him and his shortcomings at this time when I'm having a hard enough time myself."

From me to you

Do you attempt to communicate your needs to your husband or partner? Have you noticed a strain in your relationship as a result of the PPD? Journal about any communication issues you are experiencing. Write down areas in which you can talk about your expectations for him. Remember to take some time before bringing them up to consider if they are reasonable.

Depressed dad?

April 4— Today it is three months since Anastasia was born. Wow. Last night I came home from the library, and Brent wanted to talk. He'd been thinking about how I said we need therapy because he doesn't understand me and I don't understand him. He said he understands more than I think he does, and he believes it's the PPD that is tearing us apart. He told me he doesn't care about the insurance, that he wants me to get help now because he hates what this is doing to our marriage. I was just blown away by that! Then he confirmed something I've been wondering about. He wonders if this PPD and how it's affecting our marriage is making him depressed, and that's why he's been sleeping so much and has headaches. He said he's afraid to be himself, to share his worries and concerns because it might set me off or make things worse. He said he feels like he has to be a strong pillar, but he's not really one inside and that is weighing on him. He's considering quitting school again because of the financial toll and the time it takes away from helping me. I told him not to quit.

One in ten fathers experience depression after the birth of a child. When the mother has postpartum depression, that number goes up to one in two fathers who also experience depression. We had no idea about that statistic when we were in the midst of it, but looking back it makes more sense.

From me to you

Do you notice some of the indicators of depression in your spouse? If your partner is experiencing symptoms, gently encourage him to seek help as well.

Future thoughts

April 4 (continued)— I am excited (if that's the right word) to go to the DAD support group next week. It's next Wednesday, and today is Friday. I told Brent to keep checking on the insurance, and I would hang on and make the most of this group. I also suggested he talk to his friend Jerry about how to relate to a wife who is dealing with depression.

I told Brent last night as I held Anastasia, "I don't always hate being a mom." I wonder if he thought I did. I don't know what made me say it. The verse on my calendar yesterday told me that the One who called me is faithful to help me do what He's called me to: Motherhood. (I Thessalonians 5:24) Some days I am overwhelmed by everything around me. There are moments, though, when I am overwhelmed with love for my children: as I cuddle Ana or tickle Jesse, as we play or dance or laugh together, as Ana coos and smiles at me and grabs my finger.

I am excited that there will come a day when I am no longer depressed, when I can look back on this time, this journal, and see what I learned, how I grew. Until then, one minute, one hour, one day at a time.

I found that knowing there could be an end to the way I was feeling was helpful to getting me through some depressed moments. Looking back on this journal, I am looking at what I learned and how I grew, reflecting on things I would not remember unless I had written them down. So much of that year was a blur. If I think about how much I lost, sadness overwhelms me. Instead, I choose to focus on the positive that has come, and will come, from sharing my experience with others, as I am grateful to others who shared with me.

From me to you

What do you have to look forward to today? Perhaps it's a lunch date or a night out. Maybe you are thinking, like I was in this entry, about a day when you are not feeling depressed, irritable, angry, or sad. Journal about some of the things you have to look forward to in the coming days. Looking to the future can help your present mood.

Desperate measures

April 6— midnight— Sitting up, waiting for Brent to come home. Anastasia was scream-ing for ten to twenty minutes, seemingly gas pain. The problem was that nothing seemed to make her happy. Finally, out of despera-tion, I brought her downstairs and put her in the baby swing. She calmed down and fell asleep. I don't know if it was because of the swing or exhaustion. But I don't want to try to move her to bed until Brent is here to take over if she starts screaming again. I don't think I could handle that again. There I was, sitting on our bed, trying everything, crying because she was, wanting to just leave her and run away. Hearing her scream killed me. Shortly after she fell asleep, Jesse started to cry. I just said aloud, "Please God. I can't handle this," and soon Jesse calmed himself down and went back to sleep, thankfully.

It had been a decent day, dare I say okay or nearly good. Though for the first time in weeks, I didn't leave the house because I was sick, plus Brent was gone all day and night, and it's cold and yucky out. I ended up overindulging in chocolate-covered raisins at night. I really didn't have any alone time, except for this journaling and my bath and nap. Shelley from church came today and was just amazing. She helped so much. I'm so grateful. She was here from 9:15 a.m. to 4:15 p.m., running out to get a few needed items. She did the dishes, laundry, and some cleaning. She brought a strudel. So thoughtful. We had a good talk. It turns out I knew one of her daughters when she lived in our neighborhood before moving out of state. She has volunteered to come help anytime, to watch the kids and whatever. I plan to take her up on that offer. I'm so tired just thinking about the fact that I am waiting for Brent. I feel bad looking at Anastasia slumped over in the swing. So afraid to move her.

One thing I remember about the PPD is a dominant feeling of desperation. I was desperate to run away, desperate to feel better, desperate to have my life back. It was in the little things too, like wanting both kids to sleep at the same time so I could also sleep.

Ah, the baby swing. This would be the beginning of an easy solution to help when our daughter was screaming. Some parents used the washing machine spinning or the motion of the car to get their babies to sleep. I no longer cared about what "experts" said about building specific sleep habits. If she was sleeping in the swing, I let her sleep in the swing. (That being said, research shows that the safest position for a baby to sleep in is on her back, and prolonged sleep in an upright position, such as in a swing, may lead to SIDS. If this is an issue, please talk with your pediatrician for other ideas to help your baby sleep.)

From me to you

In which behaviors or indulgences do you find comfort during desperate moments? If they are generally safe, do not allow the voices of "experts" to shame you into guilt over them. Discuss them with a counselor or trusted adviser if you are unsure.

Bring it all in prayer

April 7— God, You are bigger than my depression. You desire for me to draw closer to You through this process instead of letting it push me further away. I give you all this anger, this bitterness, the overwhelmed feelings, whatever I have because I know You care for me and want to help me conquer this depression. I just want to quit. God, don't let me! How should I spend my afternoon? A nap? Try to get things done, phone calls made? I want to run away and leave it all for Brent to deal with.

As I was writing this book, I was reading through the Psalms. Psalm 5:1-3 (NLT) really connects with some of what I was feeling during PPD:

O LORD, hear me as I pray;
Pay attention to my groaning.
Listen to my cry for help, my King and my God,
For I pray to no one but you.

Listen to my voice in the morning, LORD.
Each morning I bring my requests to You and wait expectantly.

From me to you

God knows what you are experiencing. He cares about you and wants to bring you through it. Tell him how you are feeling. Affirm what you know to be true about Him from what you have read or been taught or sung in worship songs. This is all part of prayer. It may be simple, but it is powerful and will help you through the valleys of PPD.

Noticing changes

April 9— Today was the DAD support group. We will meet six times in seven weeks (next week off for the Easter holiday). Today's group helped me realize a difference the depression has made in me— I now have a hard time opening up in a group of people I don't know well. That's why I've been so hesitant to share in the "transition group" at church [for those who didn't regularly attend the mid-week service, this was a surface-level discussion group instead of a deep small group with the same people each week]. We need to pick a night to attend church and stick with it, so I can get into a small group soon. Anyway, the DAD group was definitely a safe place. I am so grateful for it. Sally, another woman there, also didn't want to be pregnant with her second. She has resentment issues. Our children are both younger (close in age). We both had difficulties in pregnancy and labor. Thank You, God, for her, for this group, and for the doctor who runs it.

The ability to see myself from the outside, as I did after attending the DAD group, was extremely helpful. I noticed I could not go deep in a discussion as a result of my depression, which was an extreme departure from my pre-PPD behavior. I resolved that something needed to be done about it, because I was unhappy with surface-level discussions. I desired to get to the heart of the matter.

From me to you

What changes in yourself have you noticed as a result of your PPD? If you are unable to objectively view yourself through the fog, ask your spouse or a trusted friend to gently point out his or her observations. Journal about these things and review them in a week or so. Some changes you may want to correct and others you may choose to allow to stay as they are. You also may wait before making a decision either way. Remember that making significant changes may not be possible in your depressed state and be willing to accept that as well.

Dealing with discouragement

April 10— Last night we noticed Jesse had a fever. He was burning up this morning—102.5°F! He woke me up crying. I quickly stripped him, gave him Tylenol and milk, then gave him a lukewarm bath. I was able to bring it down to 100.5°F. I always feel so sad when he's miserable. He seems much better now. He didn't want breakfast but he still has his milk. Brent was going to stay in bed a little longer this morning. I was going to leave Anastasia with him, so I could go grocery shopping with only one kid. But with Jesse's fever, I don't want to take him out. Now Ana just started nursing. So I am discouraged. I really wanted to get out and get to the grocery store. Maybe I can still find a way.

Upon reflection, I can see how much getting out of the house meant for me. It was so important that I was actually disappointed not to be able to go grocery shopping! Did I find a way to get to the store that day? It's not recorded in my journal, so I don't know.

But I do know that I was able to avoid sinking into a bad mood as a result because that is not recorded either. It was a personal success that I named the emotion (discouragement) and allowed myself to feel it without it taking over the rest of my day.

From me to you

When circumstances don't turn out the way you've hoped or when you are discouraged because of a change in plans that no one could anticipate, it may be helpful to talk about it or write about it. Be honest about your feelings. Pray and tell God about the disappointment. Perhaps you can try something else instead of your plans. Try to avoid allowing a setback to spiral your mood into a pity party.

Understand what you can control

April 11— Jesse had a rough time last night. I bet the ear infection is back. We have a doctor's appointment in an hour. Brent and I talked about my seeking therapy. He agrees with Lily about the necessity of having a Christian counselor, despite insurance. That's good news as I start looking. Preferably I'd want someone on our insurance plan, but I'm glad it's not needed, not the most important thing.

This morning's reading in *Conquering Depression* talked about the tools that lessen depression. The authors listed knowledge as a key: knowing the symptoms, where you can get help, and that there are Christian counselors who want to help. It was very empowering to read about the fact that I cannot control when the pain will come into my life, but I can control how long it will continue. Knowledge is an important tool in understanding how to stop the pain![9]

I will NOT GIVE UP! I will NOT GIVE UP! God wants me to overcome this illness, and I can with His help and the help of professionals. God, lead me to the right counselor. Please let the counselor be on my insurance. Please help me to take meds if that's what they think will help me. I want to honor Your method of healing me, no matter what it involves.

Here I am again, talking about control, but in a positive way. I was not trying to control outside circumstances: my child's behavior, my baby's sleep schedule, my husband's irritating habits. I was realizing that I am in control of my reactions including how long I will sit in the pain. When I wrote about knowledge helping to stop the pain, I was referring to knowing more about PPD, about my triggers, about the ways to get healthy, and also about behaviors I could try to help myself, such as finding a counselor.

Many people in my life were Christians who stressed the need to see a Christian counselor. I understand that may not be possible for everyone, or even preferred. What I really needed was a professional licensed counselor, Christian or not. While I preferred to find someone who shared my faith, the important thing was to see a therapist to walk me through my PPD.

From me to you

What things in your life are you able to control? Is there a step you need to take this week toward achieving control of that situation? Write in your journal about ways you want to take control and what outcome you hope to accomplish as a result.

Handling disappointment

April 12— Brent just told me the insurance company rejected my application after nearly a month of waiting. I am so frustrated!! Why?! He can't find out anything till Monday because today is Saturday. I wish he hadn't told me. God help me to deal with this as I don't have time to wallow or wonder. I have a home party show this afternoon.

Had a great show this afternoon and good adult interaction. I ate a lot of chocolate for some reason though.

I'm a little disappointed not to have the DAD group this week but I have the phone list. Maybe I'll call Sally from the group. Still need to work on getting out of the house alone for "me time" and finding a therapist. Need to get myself exercising again now that I'm feeling better (from the head cold). Need to get to bed earlier so getting up doesn't seem so hard!!

I want to tell this younger version of myself to hold on, that it will all work out and she will get through it, despite this setback. Seeking positive amidst the negative was beneficial. I would encourage her to continue to take steps toward her goals of exercising and getting to bed earlier for more sleep, both behaviors known to improve a depressed mood.

From me to you

When you are waiting for something, it can be hard to be patient when you're feeling your best mentally and physically. During depression, waiting seems endless. Then, if you finally receive an answer after waiting for so long and it's not what you expected, be careful not to further isolate or fall into a deeper depression. Pray. Praise God through the challenge. Write in a journal. Remember Who is ultimately in control of your situation and trust Him to bring you what you need.

Reaching out

April 14— Rough night last night as kids were up alternating every other hour it seemed. Talked with Sally from DAD today. She called to talk because her baby was screaming. I think she just needed to hear that someone else felt how she felt.

Looking back, I love that I thought about calling Sally and she ended up calling me the next day. I don't remember if I did call her the previous day, but I think I would have journaled that if I had.

From me to you

Reach out. You are not alone. It does not necessarily need to be someone going through PPD. Someone needs to hear from you, and you need the encouragement she can offer. Isolation will only deepen your depression.

Mentioning medication

April 15— Tonight Brent's friend Alex came over, and we talked about my PPD. He's bipolar. This afternoon I talked with Jill from church. She went through PPD with her last child and is still seeing a therapist. She told me what a difference her meds made. God, I ask for this insurance situation to be resolved soon and for a good doctor/therapist. Please help me to find one who is a Christian, has experience with PPD, and is on my insurance. Help me to be receptive to taking meds, if that's how I will get better.

For reasons I don't remember, I was nervous to take antidepressants. Perhaps it was the cultural stigma attached to depression or PPD. The cases that made the national news and were called "postpartum depression" involved women who were killing their children or themselves. That was both alarming and unhelpful. As mentioned in the preface, postpartum depression and postpartum psychosis are very different things. It is important for the world to understand this difference so that women can feel free to seek the help they need without fear of having their children taken away.

Being surrounded by so many people who experienced mental illness of some sort, whether related to pregnancy or not, really helped me to understand and see the truth that there is no reason to be ashamed of mental illness. Their presence in my life reminded me that, despite the lies my depression shouted into my moments of desperation, I was not alone. It also planted seeds of compassion in my heart for those who experience depression or PPD.

From me to you

Are you concerned about taking medicine to help with your PPD? Explore why you may be feeling that way. Talk with your doctor or counselor about those concerns. How can you someday be helpful to someone else who has experienced a hard time? Perhaps that thought can give you hope in your depression.

Meditate on God's Word

April 16— Zephaniah 3:17 (NLT): "For the LORD your God is living among you. He is a mighty savior. He will take delight in you with gladness. With His love, He will calm all your fears. He will rejoice over you with joyful songs."

Thank You, God, for this truth from Your Word. Help me to hold tightly to You! Help me to establish a daily quiet time of meditation on Your Word. Amen.

After this, I wrote about preparing to go to the Good Friday service at church. Depression made me feel overwhelmed by my sins, as I was by everything else around me. I wrote: "Let me be set free from their hold on me. I pray against sadness, apathy, and depression. Let me rejoice in Jesus' amazing sacrifice and hold tight to the truth that Easter is coming, as in a celebration of the resurrection." I am grateful I was not so blinded by my depression that I could not remember those truths, yet I know it can be a struggle for many others.

From me to you

Are you able to see past your own sins to the forgiveness Jesus offers by His sacrifice on the cross? Read Romans 5:6-11 and reflect on the Good News of the Gospel. What truth from God's Word means something to you today? Meditate on it. That just means thinking about it over and over again. Putting positive truth into a depressed mind can make a huge difference in your mood.

Change is hard

April 18— I looked back at my journal on that night at the library and my plans to change my reactions and interactions with Brent. I am doing better, though I still fall into the trap of criticism and anger, allowing the depression symptoms to direct me instead of my coping mechanisms. Sometimes it's easier to feel bad than to work through it. However, saying certain things and lashing out at Brent only leaves me feeling bad, too.

Doing the right thing often feels like too much work. I've found it's always worth the effort though. I have never regretted the work it took to change some aspect of my life. From losing weight to getting a college degree, anything worthwhile means time and intention. Working on the way I related to my husband would be key to a lasting marriage, which is what I wanted then and still desire today.

From me to you

When do you feel it's too hard to change? Journal about times when your effort was worth it to achieve the change you desired. Counseling can help you work through your negative patterns and behaviors, but you have to be willing to do the work.

Write daily goals

April 19— Today I began to study Job in *The Inspirational Study Bible: Life Lessons from the Inspired Word of God* (NCV). May I learn from his example, not sinning in my suffering. The verses linked to the passage which spoke to me: I Peter 5:8-9— "Refuse to give in to him (devil), by standing strong in your faith." Philippians 1:27— "Be sure that you live in a way that brings honor to the Good News of Christ." I Corinthians 15:58— "Stand strong. Do not let anything change you." (emphasis mine) God, help me to remember these passages as I struggle with PPD. I want to honor You with the way I handle these emotions and these symptoms. Show me how to live each moment, as I struggle against my depression and anger. Help me REFUSE TO GIVE IN!! I know that You want to see me through this valley. I know I can be changed by the power of Your love. Amen!

[later in the day] Today I fought my symptoms. I was able to function and get some things done around the house: making meals, laundry, unloading the dishwasher. I didn't have much stimulating adult interaction and getting out of the house was to return a video [to the movie rental place before there were digital streaming services] and go to Dairy Queen to indulge my chocolate craving. I want to start exercising again. Hoping to be able to get up tomorrow morning.

We'll see how the night goes with Ana. It's 11:30, and I'm going to sleep.

I don't know what happened that next morning. I didn't write about it. But still, I feel that having the goals, small as they were, proved to be essential in helping me toward recovery. I struggled to consistently find motivation for myself to exercise regularly and avoid feeding my sweet tooth. Yet I continued to set those as priorities by which I would try to improve my mental health.

From me to you

Take the time to write some daily goals for yourself. Make sure they are small and attainable. When you accomplish one, celebrate. If you do not get to all of them, try again tomorrow.

Being intentional

April 20— This is Easter morning and I am attempting to use the medicine of laughter to fight my depression. God's joy used to flow through me before my PPD. God, help me to rejoice in all that is around me and use laughter to help.

April 21— Today's "medicine" is touch. I am realizing that I don't like to be touched by Brent when I am depressed. But I need to allow it and touch back to break through the physical isolation of depression.

One of my books, *Conquering Depression*, mentioned types of "medicine" for the body and soul anyone could use to help ward off depressed feelings.[10] Being intentional about certain behaviors can help break down the walls which depression builds, especially the one I realized regarding touch.

From me to you

Laughter and touch can be helpful for you. Find a way to laugh today. Consider touching your spouse (or a friend) or allow yourself to be touched. Something as simple as a hand on your back or a hug can make a huge difference in your mood and break down barriers you may have unintentionally set up in your relationships.

Choosing to communicate

April 21— (continued) The rest of my day was okay, though I allowed myself to get disappointed when I got home from breakfast alone. I asked Brent to consider doing that once a week. He automatically said, "That would be really hard," especially when his school started up again for the semester. What I don't understand is why it has to be so hard. It makes me angry sometimes when he responds that way to requests. He said he'd be able to do it again sooner but couldn't commit to weekly. I told him that I needed the schedule, the routine. I am trying to assert my needs and cope with my PPD. But Brent doesn't always respond the way I hope he will. Then I get discouraged and wonder if I should bother trying again. Regarding morning baths, I've stopped asking and started telling him: "I'm taking a bath. I need you to watch the kids." Good news, the insurance got approved, so Brent said I can start to see a therapist as soon as I find one. Praise God!

April 22— Horrible fight with Brent, though I didn't yell or vent my anger. Somehow, I was able to not sin— at least that's how I see it— in my anger. I wanted to yell at him, run out of the house and leave him with the screaming baby for his yelling at me for no apparent reason. He said it was because he was in a bad mood. It just bugs me that I can't do anything right for him, I feel. And when I want to leave the house for an hour alone, he wants me to wait till the kids are asleep. Why the double standard? Why should my break come at the end of my "shift"? It's like I pull a "double" every day and get no lunch break <u>alone</u>. I need time alone!

Any illness can be rough on a marriage. It seems mental illness, due to its invisibility, may make the tough times more treacherous to wade through. With PPD, it can be a sudden change on top of an already new situation. Parenting a newborn is challenging, and balancing that with a toddler and a wife with PPD can be enough to make a husband snap. I don't hold this against my husband. I do wish we had learned better communication skills before we found ourselves in these trenches. Unfortunately, it would be a few years before we went to marriage counseling and learned to better communicate our needs and support each other.

The third medicine mentioned in *Conquering Depression* was communication. The authors say it's not easy and even compare it to taking cough medicine. However, this allows us to let someone else into our situation, to hear what we are feeling and make our depression more manageable.[11]

From me to you

What needs do you wish to communicate? What feelings do you desire to share? Are you willing to allow someone else into your situation? Be careful to communicate with a safe person. Knowing who is safe to talk to when you are in a fragile mental state is essential. Not everyone will understand what you are going through and offer help.

Cling to God

April 25— Last night Brent told me he felt God wanted him to give me this message: *Be intentional about clinging to God, and He will restore the joy to my life.* I had just been praying about joy last week. So, thankfully, I'm up and the kids aren't yet so I'm able to have some time to myself. I asked him about the once a week, and he said he could do that, just couldn't guarantee the day, unless it was Thursday, which is when I have a playgroup for Jesse. So I can get half of what I need. Be flexible!

I just read Isaiah 42:16 (NCV): "Then I will lead the blind along a way they never knew; I will guide them along paths they have not known. I will make the darkness become light for them, and the rough ground smooth. These are the things I will do; I will not leave my people."

God, thank You that You will not abandon me. Thank You for reminding me about Your faithfulness and love!

Conquering Depression's medicine of communication also mentions prayer, talking to God.[12] I was raised in a faith tradition which encouraged open communication with God as my Heavenly Father, so prayer came naturally to me as an expression of my faith. Many times I found that being able to communicate with God brought me through rough times in my PPD.

From me to you

Is prayer hard for you? There is not a formula you are required to follow. There are no magic words to be said. A prayer can be as simple as "Help!" or it can be a lengthy pouring out of your heart.

Remember that God is with those who follow Him. Pray the words of Psalm 130 (NLT) to get started:

> From the depths of despair, O LORD,
>   I call for Your help.
> Hear my cry, O LORD.
>   Pay attention to my prayer.
> LORD, if You kept a record of our sins,
>   who, O LORD, could ever survive?
> But You offer forgiveness,
>   that we might learn to fear You.
> I am counting on the LORD;
>   yes, I am counting on Him.

I have put my hope in His word.
I long for the LORD
    more than sentries long for the dawn,
    yes, more than sentries long for the dawn.
O Israel, hope in the LORD;
    for with the LORD there is unfailing love.
    His redemption overflows.
He himself will redeem Israel
    from every kind of sin.

Despair, cry for help, pray. Forgiveness, hope, longing. God's love is unfailing. Amen!

Try journaling

April 27— In today's devotion from *Conquering Depression*, the importance of the journal is noted. This has been such an important part of bringing me closer to healing. I reached out and got a few counseling referrals, too. I need to write down what I want to ask and then get on the phone. God help me to do that, even as I juggle home, my home party business, and the kids.

I have kept diaries or journals since my elementary school years. As I grew older, the entries were more intentional and eventually morphed into a combination prayer and Bible study place to write along with what I was experiencing in my daily life. I have found that this method is more accurately a reflection of who I am and what I am going through.

From me to you

If you haven't journaled your feelings and experience yet, I highly recommend this practice. There are no rules that you need to follow. Just write the truth. It doesn't have to be elegant or poetic. You've read my words and know that there were just moments that it was all I could do to pick up the pen and write. Write just for you. No one ever has to read it. The process of writing will bring you clarity and help lead you on the path of healing.

Problems with procrastination

April 28— All I seem to do is talk about seeing a therapist. Now that I'm able to do so, what am I waiting for? Am I afraid of something? I've been feeling better and more capable, even as I struggle with feeling down. But maybe I'm doing better than I thought. Maybe I'm past the worst. Then Anastasia starts screaming or Brent does something I don't want, and I get angry. If nothing else, I need to deal with that issue. Making time for it hasn't been a priority though.

Today Cara called and suggested we meet at the park. So I changed my plans. I'm so glad I did, but it was one way I've kept myself from making the calls. I've also been trying to make my business calls for the end of the month. So I've done that the past two afternoons instead of napping or anything else. Nights get taken over by the kids. Last night Brent wasn't home and tonight he was doing homework. Tomorrow night is a business meeting for me. So any calls will have to be made again in the afternoon. I've also wanted to take time for goal setting (mentioned in one of my books) and deeper personal reflection, to go through *This Isn't What I Was Expecting* and some of its questions. When can I get all this done? Certainly not now, at 10:54 p.m.! I want to read my *Conquering Depression* devotional and get some sleep before Ana wants to eat again. (Later, after I read it, I wrote the following:) Talk about God's timing. Tonight's devotional was on the importance of finding a Christian counselor. My goal is to make the phone calls this week. God, help me!

What if I didn't like the counselor? What if she didn't like me? What would a counselor tell me? What if my PPD could not be helped? What hard changes would I be required to make to really benefit from counseling? As I have been learning in recent months (seriously, I love that God continues to teach us as we seek Him), procrastination can stem from fear and from perfectionism, both of which I can see were in my mindset as I wrote those words in my journal.

From me to you

Do you procrastinate? If so, can you identify what is holding you back? It can be easier to stay stuck, even when you've longed for a change. What if the change is not what you were hoping it would be? What if the counselor does not help? The "what-ifs" can get you stuck in a negative thought spiral if you are not careful. However, to experience true change, it's imperative to take a chance and make an attempt, even if it's not perfect. Allow some discomfort today if it may possibly lead to a better tomorrow.

Sleepless night

April 29— What a horrible night. I was so <u>angry</u> at Anastasia for continuing to wake me up. At 2 a.m. I understood, but then at 4?! I fell asleep nursing her and tried to put her back in her crib at 5. She just cried. Then Jesse cried, and I grabbed her and brought her back into my room. I practically tossed her on the bed and angrily changed her diaper and kept shoving her pacifier in her mouth. She wouldn't stop screaming. I finally gave in and laid her in bed and nursed her some more.

I was angry because Brent wasn't up, dealing with this. He was sleeping. I was angry because I wanted him to take care of her. Woke up again at 6:30 and tried to put her in the bassinet. As soon as I laid back down, she started to cry. I was so angry. Then Brent started snoring, so I nudged him until he stopped. She kept crying, and I started kicking my legs and burying my head in the pillow. I just wanted some uninterrupted sleep!

Is that too much to ask?! Then Brent asked me what was wrong, and I snapped, "She just won't leave me alone!" I got up and ran into the bathroom. I turned on the fan, so I wouldn't have to hear her cry. I used the toilet and felt guilty for every second I was in there, letting her cry. I hoped Brent would take care of her.

When I came back to the bedroom, he was gone, and she was still crying. Then he came in and stood by the bassinet as if he would pick her up. I angrily brushed past him, turned off the morning alarm, which was set to go off in 15 minutes, and threw her over my shoulder. Once I sat down with her, she burped loudly and I think she tooted, too. She also ate well. I was just so <u>frustrated</u>!! Brent was in bed asleep again. Lucky! God, help me to manage these angry thoughts in a way that honors you.

I cried as I relived that morning through the journal entry. Just a few days earlier I thought I was doing okay. Depression is tricky like that. I felt the desperation in my actions as if it were yesterday. My heart broke for that young mother who just wanted to get some sleep. Counselors encourage those experiencing mental illness to get enough sleep, but they seem to forget what life is like with a newborn, especially a fussy one.

From me to you

When your sleep is interrupted, how do you react? Have you noticed a correlation between your PPD symptoms and a lack of sleep? Write about your experience. What can you do to get past a rough night? Think of a simple act of self-care to tend to your needs and try it the next time this comes up for you.

Anchored by faith

April 29— (continued) I commit to beginning the phone calls in search of a counselor to-day. Help me to keep that commitment. Make the time— I will do it when Jesse goes down for his nap. I know I have a lot of other things I want or need to get done during that time. Lord, help me to make the best use of that time. Soon Jesse will be getting up for the day. Help me to make the most of this time I have now with Your Word.

"You must give your whole heart to Him (God) and hold out your hands to Him for help. Put away the sin that is in your hand; let no evil remain in your tent. Then you can lift up your face without shame, and you can stand strong without fear." —Job 11:13-15 (NCV) I know this is one of Job's friends telling him that his troubles stem from hidden sin, but it seems to speak to me this morning.

Through Brent, God, You have told me to be intentional in clinging to You and You will restore joy to my life. Lord, help me to do just that. I am doing it right now. Please bless these efforts this morning. Help me to lift up my face without shame and stand strong without fear. Keep sin out of my house. May I be without sin for just a moment. I know I sin so many times throughout my day. It is impossible to be blameless in Your sight, God, if not for the blood of Jesus which covers over my sin. Because of that blood, I can overcome the slavery to sin. This PPD has made the struggle all the worse, as I feel trapped, ineffective. It's hard to go on with my daily activities when I have a night/morning like I just did. Help me, Holy Spirit, to conquer my depression today. Help me to fight off angry thoughts, outbursts, tiredness, sugar/starch cravings, hopelessness, sadness, and my desire to escape this all. Help me to overcome and conquer this depression.

"(God) does everything just right and on time, but people can never completely understand what He is doing." Ecclesiastes 3:11 (NCV) God's thoughts and ways are unlike mine (Isaiah 55:8-9). Help me to remember this truth and not question it. The final verse in my study of Job today struck a chord, saying people only feel the pain in their bodies and feel sorry for themselves. (Job 14:22). Lord, let me not be oblivious to all that is around me. Let me not pity myself. My hope is You! Amen

I had experienced a difficult night without sleep. My reactions were angry (see previous entry). I continued to seek God, though, and that's really what brought me through my desperate moments. I cannot even imagine what it would have been like for me to go through PPD without my faith in God. Even when I doubted or my faith was shaken, I returned to God and His Word. His promises kept me anchored.

From me to you

If you don't know God, seek Him in his Word. Ask a pastor or a friend you know who attends church. God wants a relationship with you, but He will not force you. He waits for you to come to Him. Even if you're uncertain about what you believe about God, you can call out to Him, possibly something as basic as, "God, I have heard about You and want to know You for myself. Help me to find You." Matthew 7:7 encourages that if you seek, you will find. "Seek the LORD while He may be found; call on Him while He is near." (Isaiah 55:6) Also James writes, "Come close to God, and God will come close to you." James 4:8a (NLT) This is a prayer God loves to answer.

Big picture thinking

April 30— Last night Brent said to me, "Tomorrow will be better" and when I asked why, he said, "Because it's tomorrow." He gave me the encouragement to see beyond the pit I was in last night. I remembered his words this morning, and so far, it is better. Though it is raining outside, which I wish wasn't so. But today is Wednesday: support group, visit with Jamie, church (the midweek service in the evening). It has to be a better day! In my Bible devotion this morning, Billy Graham referred to the blind man born that way in John 9 and the disciples' question of sin. He explained that Jesus encouraged the disciples to see how suffering could bring glory to God.[13]

"And after you suffer for a short time, God, who gives all grace, will make everything right. He will make you strong and support you and keep you from falling." I Peter 5:10a (NCV)

God, I know that in the grand scheme of my life, this suffering is only for a little while. Help me to find the right counselor to lead me through this valley and to see the support You offer me.

Two things jump off the page at me as I re-read this entry. I chose to study Job and his suffering. What I was experiencing, when compared to what he went through, was indeed light and momentary. He lost his seven sons, three daughters, 7,000 sheep, 3,000 camels, 500 yoke of oxen, 500 female donkeys, and many servants, all in one day. Then soon after, though we don't know exactly when, he was covered in painful boils from the soles of his feet to the crown of his head. His wife foolishly advised him to curse God and die (Job 2:9). Yet despite all of this pain, loss, agony, and adversity, Job did not sin with his lips (2:10). How many times already had my words been sinful, not to even mention my actions and thoughts?

My husband was absolutely correct. Tomorrow is a new day. True, things can be worse, but today, in this moment, we don't know that. Why waste energy worrying about what may come tomorrow? It cannot help us; it only hurts.

Jesus said, "Do not worry about your life, what you will eat or drink; or about your body, what you will wear. Is not life more than food, and the body more than clothes? ... Can any one of you by worry-ing add a single hour to your life? ... Your heavenly father knows that you need them. But seek first His kingdom and His righteousness, and all these things will be given to you as well. Therefore do not worry about tomorrow, for tomorrow will worry about it-self. Each day has enough trouble of its own." (from Matthew 6:25-34) As I consider again these wise words of Jesus, I am reminded of the importance of spending time in sound Biblical teaching.

From me to you

Do you believe that tomorrow will be better? Do you find it hard to look toward the big picture? How do you feel about the suffering you are experiencing? Write in your journal about these things. Then seek God and His truth in the Bible. Any amount of time you put towards this will make a difference in your life and in your depression.

Avoid adding to your depression

May 1— Another difficult day. It's been hard today, including insurance issues. Dr. Hamm, the therapist I found, may not be on it. She said she was; the company says she's not. Brent's going to look into it tomorrow. All these things seem to pile up. Brent didn't get the job. [We had been hoping for something more stable and creative for him; he interviewed for a position he wanted and it didn't happen.] We're unsure where to go from here. Why did he feel so strongly that God wanted him to pursue it, only to not get it? To tell him it's time to look for another job? Just to see if he would be obedient? Why?

I had a hard time in general today, just an overwhelming sense of blah— sadness, irritability, hopelessness, tiredness. Last night I told Brent I needed to get out for a little while tonight. So I'm at Panera Bread, enjoying a delicious soup and sandwich. It's so nice to be alone. And to focus on my life, my healing from this depression. God, help me to work through the issues I've been putting off.

In today's *Conquering Depression* study, I am challenged about my many bad habits. I know I need to change, but part of me doesn't want to. It's easier not to do anything. God, help me to fight that evil one who would have me stuck in this depression!

Do I engage in some activities that tend to make me depressed?

I recently met a friend through our shared tragedy of experiencing a house fire. Kelly's fire was a total loss. She and her family lost everything, including a family pet. She immersed herself in reading about World War II. When I asked her why, she told me it was because she realized that even as bad as her current experience was, it could be so much worse. She found hope in those stories, and she still enjoys them years later.

From me to you

Did you realize that there are activities you are doing that could add to your depression? It may seem like mindless entertainment, but gauge how you feel after watching a certain TV program or reading a certain type of book. I will share more about this in the next entry.

Read (or watch) what inspires you or helps you through. I found it helpful to read about other people's experiences with depression to understand what I was going through. (See Further Reading for some suggestions.) Find truth to hold on to as you rebuild or recover from your PPD.

Ready for revision

May 1— (continued) Television: I know I watch way too much! It started during my second pregnancy, when I was supposed to rest all the time. Breaking the bad habit of the amount I watch will be hard. Lord, help me. I know some television is just serving to neutralize my brain. I need to avoid sad, weepy stuff, which I mostly do. Last week I surprised myself by losing it in tears at the end of "ER" when Carter's grandma died (on the show). Tonight's episode is going to have her funeral. Can I watch it the way I'm feeling? I honestly don't know. I want to, but I know I shouldn't. Can I distance myself from it enough to not let it affect me? Other shows I just watch to fill time or to indulge a "guilty pleasure." I will no longer watch these on my own. Same with "Law & Order," which is a brilliant show, but it involves death and so much that I don't need in my life right now. The news: I need to make certain not to watch more than an hour a day. It's too much for me to take right now, all the death and bad news. I will stop having it on for background noise. Unless there is something specific I want to see, I will turn it off or let Jesse watch a video.

Help me to replace the viewing time with something <u>more positive</u> and <u>less passive</u>. Listen to worship and Christian music, even classical or other instrumental songs. I need positive influences. Instead of plopping on the couch and just seeing what's on, I could be intentional about having quiet time, which I struggle to find. Even just listening to the music while I sit there is better. I don't need all those commercial messages attacking me while I nurse Anastasia or fold laundry or play with Jesse or cook dinner. This change will be huge. Help me to make it, God. This is my biggest area of a change I need to make and feel prepared to make. Help me to start using my mind instead of allowing TV to fill it with nonsense.

Reading those words in which I identified what I was allowing into my mind sparked a feeling of happy pride for my past self. The word "revising" is defined by Merriam-Webster as looking over again in order to correct or improve. I saw something in my life that needed to be revised. I knew I was able to change it despite my depressed mindset, so I committed to doing it. This would make a world of difference for me then and in the years to come.

From me to you

What behaviors in your life do you need to revise? Identify what bad habits may be contributing to your mood and commit to cut them out if you are able. Maybe you could replace them with some of the positive activities I suggested to myself in the journal entry. It will feel like coming up for a breath of air after being underwater for too long.

A loose schedule

May 1— (continued) I had been telling Brent my desperate need for a schedule right now— for me, for the kids. I must identify what should be on it and then stick to it. Instead of waiting for another time, let's do it right now! [I wrote out times for waking up, showering, eating, feeding my newborn, naps, play time, couple time, and bedtime.] There's one day. Can I stick to that? It's pretty simple, yet structured. I see my need to plan for dinner ahead of time. Maybe I can do that during some alone time— plan the week's meals and activities, groceries, etc. I want to fit in time for Jesse to do specific things, such as color pictures or read stories. I want to fit in specifics for me, too, including exercise and self-development. Help me to do this.

When feeling overwhelmed by PPD, I found it helpful to have a loose schedule. It allowed me to know what was coming in my day, as well as permitted me the eyes to see what was missing, such as specific activities for my toddler or even planning dinner. These days, when too much is going on in my life, I often take the time to write out a loose schedule of my planned activities or goals I want to accomplish for the day or week. This action allows me more control over my time and helps me achieve the important goals I have.

From me to you

Do you have a daily schedule? What things would you like to accomplish in a day? Writing down something simple, as I did, may help you take control over one area of your life. The key is to make it flexible and not to be hard on yourself if you do not stick to it. If you consider the schedule to be a tool to help you instead of a task master to control you, it can be very helpful. You will give your mood a boost as you accomplish such tasks as "shower" or "make dinner."

Rest in God

May 5— Last two nights have been horrible with Ana, and the lack of sleep causes me to be more depressed and quick to anger. God help me to get some good sleep now. Amen.

This short journal entry reminds me of one of David's psalms. He was in a desperate situation, yet he knew his need for God and wrote these words of comfort we can repeat today: "On my bed I remember You; I think of You through the watches of the night. Because You are my help, I sing in the shadow of Your wings. I cling to You; Your right hand upholds me." (Psalm 63:6-8)

From me to you

Tiredness can contribute to irritability. Find ways to sneak in a nap if you are able. The housework can wait. If you have not been getting enough rest, your mood will suffer.

Sweet slumber

May 6— So glad to be out by myself right now. The kids are with Roberta, and I'm at a park, enjoying the nice weather. Last night was horrible. I laid in bed a little after 9, trying to fall asleep. Brent was at his mom's watching hockey [we didn't have cable, so she allowed him to come over and watch it in a separate room]. Twenty minutes into trying to sleep, Anastasia starts crying. Don't remember if she was gassy, or wet diaper, or what. I tried everything to get her back to sleep. Finally, just before 11, while I was using the computer, she fell asleep in my arms. When I put her in the crib, she woke up and cried. Then Jesse started crying, too. After five minutes it was too much for me to take, and I called Brent and asked him to come home. Ana fell asleep while I comforted Jesse. I put him down then went to the bathroom. Brent came home and the crying began again. I just looked at Brent, went into the bedroom, and closed the door. For an hour, I drifted in and out of sleep, only to hear Jesse crying. So I went to Brent and asked what he'd tried. He told me he was mad about the way I'd "handed" Jesse over to him. When I asked if he still was mad, he said, "No." I gave him a suggestion to give Jesse some milk, and I went back to bed. I woke up a little later to hear Brent burping Anastasia. Don't know when that was. Maybe 2? Anyway, not another peep from either of them until 6:30 when I heard Anastasia. So I got up and fed her and started my day, better rested than the previous two nights. Thank You, God.

When I could no longer handle things on my own, I sought help from my husband. Here's some truth from Ecclesiastes 4:9-12 to consider:

Two are better than one,
    because they have a good return for their labor:
If either of them falls down, one can help the other up.
But pity anyone who falls and has no one to help them up.
Also, if two lie down together, they will keep warm.
    But how can one keep warm alone?
Though one may be overpowered,
    two can defend themselves.
A cord of three strands is not quickly broken.

From me to you

If you don't have a spouse or partner, do you have someone you can call for help in moments like this? Find a trustworthy family member, friend, or neighbor to help carry the burden when it becomes too much. Waking up feeling rested is worth the effort involved to achieve it.

God will use this

May 6— (continued) God's power is made perfect in my weakness. Hallelujah! He wants to use this for His glory, to draw others to Him. Holy Spirit, help me to speak about my struggles and victories when You prompt me to, so that I may bring You glory. Use this for Your good!

God does always want what's best for me, but the problem comes when I misinterpret what that means— His plans are different from mine. He sees the large picture and what we really need to bring His ultimate plan to fruition: that all might be saved. God wants me to use my life experiences for His glory. His plan is the one that is in "operation." Help me to see through Your perspective, Lord. Jesus suffered so much more than I do, and He saw it as part of the Greater Plan. Help me to cling to You as I weather this depression. Amen.

I have always felt that I was to use my experience with PPD for God's glory, to encourage others and draw them to Him. That has been my prayer for you as you read this book, no matter where you are in your PPD or other depression. Trust Him to use your situation, too.

From me to you

When the situation finds you worn down, cry out to Jesus. He is faithful to help you through, despite how you feel about the situation. Try to think of a time when you thought you were at your end but suddenly you were able to forge ahead and overcome the trial. Write about it in your journal. Talk about it with a friend. You may be used by God to bring much needed encouragement to another person.

When setbacks arise

May 7— Since we now have the insurance, I finally got a prescription from my doctor, and I just took my first Zoloft.

Dr. Hamm saw me this morning. She is a licensed clinical social worker and suffered PPD herself. Anyway, according to her test, I am 1 point under a "severe depression." I have been getting worse, waiting to see someone. Brent and I will meet with her Monday night, and then we'll figure out how often I will see her. I felt very comfortable with her once I got past the horrible start to the morning. She's not in my insurance plan. That sent me over the edge sobbing. But Brent and I had said before that insurance wasn't the most important factor— being a Christian with PPD experience ranked higher. So we will go further into debt. God help us know what to do about our financial difficulties. Lead Brent to a new job or bring him lots of insurance policies, <u>please</u>. [He sold insurance at this time.] Continue to bless my home party business.

God can use my depression for good—the "cracks" in my life can make something beautiful in His hands! Amen

May 10— I still can't believe what happened after all that. Dr. Hamm called me up and said she couldn't fit me into her schedule and tried to get me to see her associate. Schedules didn't work for us. I just don't understand why she even saw me in the first place. So I have a new therapist to see in a week from Monday. Jill at church goes to her, Dr. Smyth. And she's really close to home, on my insurance plan, etc.

Tomorrow is Mother's Day, and I really want Brent to acknowledge me and make me feel special. I'm sure he didn't do anything, and I'll try not to be disappointed.

Re-reading those journal entries together reminds me of many things. I asked God to help us with our financial difficulties. When Dr. Hamm was not on our insurance, suddenly she was unable to fit me into her schedule. While that was beyond my understanding at the time, I now see how He paved the way for me to see someone else who was paid for by insurance. I still remember meeting Dr. Hamm and then getting the phone call that she couldn't fit me in. At the time I remember thinking that was inexcusable to do to someone in my mental state, and I felt it was very unprofessional. Then I see Dr. Smyth's name, and I remember that she was a good fit for me. The meds also started to make a difference in my mood. I want to tell my past self, "Hang on! Help is on the way!"

I am also reminded that God cares about the little things in our lives, as well as the big ones. Romans 5:1-5 (NLT) encourages me to view these setbacks and difficulties differently:

> Therefore, since we have been made right in God's sight by faith, we have peace with God because of what Jesus Christ our Lord has done for us. Because of our faith, Christ has brought us into this place of undeserved privilege where we now stand, and we confidently and joyfully look forward to sharing God's glory. We can rejoice, too, when we run into problems and trials, for we know that they help us develop endurance. And endurance develops strength of character, and character strengthens our confident hope of salvation. And this hope will not lead to disappointment. For we know how dearly God loves us, because he has given us the Holy Spirit to fill our hearts with his love.

These setbacks were building up my endurance, which would work on my character and, in turn, my hope. That would ultimately continue to guide me

through the other challenges I would face in the years
to come.

From me to you

How do you react to setbacks and challenges?
Do you believe that perseverance can help you de-
velop your character? Yes, persevering through difficult times is so much harder when depressed. However, it's something to strive towards because it will
help pull you out of the downward spiral.

Examine your emotions

May 11— Brent surprised me with a beautiful bouquet of roses for Mother's Day. It was nice that he did something. I'm not sure if it's the meds or just the way things are going, but I haven't struggled too much in the past few days. Tonight Anastasia's crying and vomiting annoyed me but didn't anger me like it might have before. I hope this is a step in the right direction. I realized that I resent Brent's staying up late and sleeping in. He doesn't have to do any middle-of-the-night feedings; he doesn't have to do breakfast in the morning. In fact, he's not "on call" like I am, and I resent that. Hopefully I can work through these feelings in therapy. I am still overwhelmed by housework and sleepiness. Took a nap today and was also able to make it to the grocery store with just Jesse because Brent was home sick. That's a frustration, one that I think all women share: When he is sick, it's like he can barely do anything. He didn't want to finish putting Jesse to bed because he didn't "feel" up to it. When I'm sick, it doesn't matter how I feel; I still have to take care of the kids. To his credit, he did unload the dishwasher today. Well, I plan to continue to examine these emotions. I still wonder if he's a little depressed. God, help us through this. Amen.

The fog was starting to clear. While I was frustrated and annoyed, unbridled anger was nowhere to be seen. I may have been frustrated with my husband, but it did not send me over the edge as it would have previously. With clarity comes the ability to see beyond emotions and reactions.

From me to you

Write out your emotions and successes you have. It will encourage you as you look back and see how you overcame unhealthy patterns. Talk through it in counseling or with a wise, trusted friend.

Bible study benefits

May 13— "You know that in the past you were living in a worthless way, a way passed down from the people who lived before you. But you were saved from that useless life. You were bought, not with something that ruins, like gold or silver, but with the precious blood of Christ, who was like a pure and perfect lamb." I Peter 1:18-19 (NCV)

This is God's truth to me— I am not worthless. I am redeemed and I am a daughter of the Most High God! Hallelujah!

God never forgets me, who I am and what I am facing! He is always with me. I must keep my eyes on Him, not my circumstances. His power can change my situation when He thinks it's time. And He, my heavenly Father, will take care of me no matter what!! Amen.

In this journal entry, the Holy Spirit led me to read something I needed to hold on to for my situation. Bible study during PPD does not have to be very long, methodical, or academic. It can be as simple as a daily devotional with a verse on each page and a short reflection. Even a verse of the day calendar can provide a means for Bible study.

From me to you

What truth do you need to hear from God's Word today? Find a short devotional (I recommend some in Further Reading) and use it as a starting point. Pick up your Bible and choose a book to read. If you don't know where to start, I recommend Psalms for the encouraging, prayer-like passages you will find. They are mostly short enough to read in just a few minutes, too.

New perspective

May 15— It's been more than a week on the Zoloft, and I'm feeling so much better. How I wish I'd done this two months ago. But everything for a reason. I have gone through such a valley. I have a new understanding of depression and a new compassion for those who experience it. I still have issues to work out, so I look forward to seeing this therapist on Monday. Now I fear feeling like I did before. And I am reminded that there will be bad days. But I can handle them with what I have learned in *Conquering Depression* and through clinging to God, who loves me no matter what. Amen.

While it would have been so much better for me if I had been able to take the antidepressants earlier in my PPD journey, I also appreciated that God could use my weakness for His glory. I was able to see things differently, without the fog of PPD. This verse encourages me and I hope it encourages you, too: "That is why, for Christ's sake, I delight in weaknesses, in insults, in hardships, in persecutions, in difficulties. For when I am weak, then I am strong." (2 Corinthians 12:10)

From me to you

What different seasons are you experiencing right now? Consider the words of Ecclesiastes 3:1-8:

There is a time for everything,
  and a season for every activity under the heavens:
a time to be born and a time to die,
a time to plant and a time to uproot,
a time to kill and a time to heal,
a time to tear down and a time to build,
a time to weep and a time to laugh,
a time to mourn and a time to dance,
a time to scatter stones and a time to gather them,
a time to embrace and a time to refrain from embracing,
a time to search and a time to give up,
a time to keep and a time to throw away,
a time to tear and a time to mend,
a time to be silent and a time to speak,
a time to love and a time to hate,
a time for war and a time for peace.

No longer reacting

May 19— Still feeling good. I have the strength now to take charge of my reactions to situations. When I find myself getting upset over the way Brent does something, I choose to not let it get to me and instead do what I want. Like yesterday. It was a gorgeous day. After church Brent was exhausted (as usual). I found myself getting annoyed. He was going to waste the day in bed. So I decided to take a picnic with the kids. We had a great time. And I felt more in control of my emotions than I have in months!

I am so proud of this young mother who took charge of her situation. She learned coping skills and chose to do something instead of reacting as she would have in past similar situations. Counseling and medication will get us part of the way; we have to do the rest.

From me to you

What are you proud of that you've done differently? Celebrate it. Record it in your journal or tell a trusted confidant. You are making positive changes in your life, and it is good to acknowledge this accomplishment!

Trusting in trials

May 26— Still feeling very good. So much more like me. I've been able to take pleasure in my kids and in time with Brent. I've been better equipped to deal with adversity. Today we received more bills from medical stuff. I have no idea how we're going to pay them! It's got me feeling a little down. But I am reminded that God is in control. Somehow He will see us through this. Just wish I knew how! God, give us wisdom to know how to make it through this situation, how to get out of this hole we're in. Please bless Brent's job to bring in money, so we can pay our bills. Amen.

Money troubles when you're thinking clearly can be difficult. During depression, it is even harder to see a way through. I chose to trust God to provide for us and guide us through this trial.

From me to you

What trial could you trust God to help you through today? Consider the beginning of Psalm 40:

> I waited patiently for the LORD to help me,
>   and He turned to me and heard me cry.
> He lifted me out of the pit of despair,
>   out of the mud and the mire.
> He set my feet on solid ground
>   and steadied me as I walked along.
> He has given me a new song to sing,
>   a hymn of praise to our God.
> Many will see what He has done and be amazed.
>   They will put their trust in the LORD.

(verses 1-3 NLT)

Appreciating my baby

May 29— I will remember to <u>always trust in God</u>, no matter what my emotional state may be at the moment! God, thank You for this reminder and the example of David (in the Bible). He knew to trust in You, despite his feelings. Help me to do the same today. I commit to You to spend daily time growing closer to You, through reading, study, prayer, and worship. Help me to be able to spend the time with You that will help me grow to know You again. May my life reflect Your Will to those around me and may I come to know You intimately as I did at the times You spoke so clearly to me. Continue to bring Your JOY into my life. Thank You for the difference I have noticed in my life since taking the medication! You are so faithful! Thank You! Also thank You for the miracle that is Anastasia— the one I didn't want at the time but is more than I could've asked for. Thank You!

I love that I can look back and observe the moment I finally could see what a miracle my precious baby girl was in my life. Now a teenager, she knows about my PPD experience; I've been very open with her about it. I have also told her if I had to go through it all again to have her as my daughter, I would do it without hesitation. In those first months of the haze, I could never have thought that. Unable to see clearly, I was beaten down by my depression. My mind, my heart, my everything— it was overwhelming beyond imagination. I am grateful I wrote these words in my journal in the midst of it all.

From me to you

How do you feel about your baby? Be honest with yourself. No one else needs to know. Are there moments, like I experienced above, in which you can appreciate your little one? Journal any thoughts you have on this topic.

Fear no evil

May 30— God allows circumstances which are difficult to enter our lives. But He does not leave us alone: "So don't worry, because I am with you. Don't be afraid, because I am your God. I will make you strong and will help you; I will support you with my right hand that saves you." Isaiah 41:10 (NCV)

How wonderful to know fear is unnecessary because I have a guide through the unknown. The Holy Spirit sheds light on the darkness and helps me to see, so I don't fear!

Reading the Bible helped put truths like the above verse in front of me on a regular basis. Sometimes I memorized them; other times I wrote them down on index cards or sticky notes to keep them easily accessible. Fear can be paralyzing during PPD, and this helped me combat those feelings.

From me to you

I encourage you to find Scripture to speak to where you are right now. Post it on a mirror or the refrigerator door. Read it aloud; make it a prayer. Remember that God says we have a faithful shepherd in Him and therefore we have no reason to fear. Check out Psalm 23 and consider its relevance to your life right now:

The LORD is my shepherd, I lack nothing.
He makes me lie down in green pastures,
He leads me beside quiet waters,
He refreshes my soul.
He guides me along the right paths
for His name's sake.
Even though I walk
through the darkest valley,
I will fear no evil,
for You are with me;
Your rod and Your staff,
they comfort me.
You prepare a table before me
in the presence of my enemies.
You anoint my head with oil;
my cup overflows.
Surely Your goodness and love will follow me
all the days of my life,

and I will dwell in the house of the LORD
forever.

Joyful

June 2— Feeling so much better has been such a change that I'm honestly surprised when I start to feel down. But so far I've been mostly able to fight it off. I have not felt "depressed" in weeks. I am able to enjoy my family again. I no longer want to run away from my kids, and Anastasia's screaming— when it occurs— is manageable for me (not grating on me or causing me to cry). Now I cry as a result of overwhelming joy when I watch Jesse "love at" his sister (give her hugs and kisses). Brent and I made love for the first time since before Ana was <u>born</u> (five months!). I feel able to serve others more. I pray for guidance in what my role in serving at church should be. God, thank You for bringing back joy in my life. I continue to cling to You, for I know You are the source of my joy! God, I am so grateful that You are a fair judge. But I am so thankful for Your grace as well and Your mercy. You are good!

In the above journal entry, I am vulnerable about some of the good changes which occurred in my life as the depression lifted. I was allowing the "medicines" of laughter and touch to work throughout my life. As my depression started to lessen, I was even considering how I might be able to help others.

From me to you

When have you most recently experienced joy? Journal about your experience. Remember you are not alone. You will get through this. Are you remembering the power of laughter, touch, and communication to help you in your PPD? If you are beginning to feel better, have you thought about how you might be able to help others around you?

Time for practical application

June 2 (continued)— I am still concerned about Brent. He hasn't been sleeping well— or some nights at all! I want to help him, but he is resistant. Talking with Dr. Smyth, my therapist, has helped me see some things. He chooses things, and I can choose how I react to his decisions: morning wake-up, perfectionist actions, etc. She has given me some tools to make my decisions. I have not been getting angry since talking with her about these things. I feel more equipped. I saw her two weeks in a row, and now we're stretching it to two weeks before I see her. It's still a month before I can get in to see the psychiatrist. Tomorrow I see Dr. Anderson for my annual OB/GYN exam and to discuss birth control. I am hesitant to go back on a pill because of my depression and prior high blood pressure. I ask for wisdom in this Lord. I am also confused about our financial situation. What should we do? God, give us direction as to how to get out of this debt and honor You!

Now that the doctor had me on an antidepressant that was clearing up the mental fog which resulted from PPD, it was time to think about how to handle challenges in my marriage, with my health, and with our financial situation. A good counselor aided me by offering new ways to look at the old problems, to focus on the heart of the issues instead of the mess of emotions and reactionary behavior, and to move into healthy behaviors instead. My husband and I did not do marital counseling at this time, but I see now that it would have been beneficial to have a third party to help us work through our recurring situations.

From me to you

Have you been seeing a counselor? What issues are you starting to work toward resolving in your life? Do you think marital counseling would be helpful for you? Journal about these things.

Hopeful

June 17— "The eyes of the LORD are on those who fear Him, on those whose hope is in His unfailing love." Psalm 33:18
My hope is You, Jesus!

Two weeks elapsed in between the previous entry and this one. They are growing further apart because I was not feeling the need to vent. While I wish I would have written more, I also realized this symbolizes the dramatic change in my emotional and mental well being.

From me to you

If you have been journaling through your PPD, go back and see how far you have come since you started. If you have not, consider starting now, wherever you are in the journey. Where do you find hope in your life today? Write about that.

Make a list

June 22— List of attainable goals I can work toward that will help me conquer depression:

1. Take my prescribed Zoloft every day.
2. Work to lose weight by eating less (and better!) and by exercising.
3. See Dr. Smyth every two weeks to work through communication issues, etc., to improve my self-thinking and my relationships.
4. Have quiet time daily— read some of my Bible, read *Conquering Depression*, read *Walk Daily with Jesus*, worship, pray (any combo of the above).
5. Get out of the house daily.
6. Continue to be open and talk about my PPD with others.
7. Inform others about PPD through an article [I was trained as a journalist and thought I might write a newspaper article].

8. Continue to attend the DAD support group if it starts again.
9. Continue to read and be informed about my PPD.
10. Attend church and be in fellowship.
11. Go to bed by 11 p.m. every night to get sleep.
12. Get out and enjoy the weather!

I like to-do lists. I always have. I'm not one to draw up really fancy lists, but having a simple plan helps me to see what I want or need to accomplish. Now that I was feeling so much better, I took my love of lists and made an action plan for myself in my journal. This was something I could reference when I found myself having a down mood swing to see if I needed to reassess my goals or redirect my path.

From me to you

Making a list of goals and plans can help you see past your current situation. Take some time and write down in your journal a few things you hope to accomplish to support your healing from PPD.

Giving thanks

June 24— Still doing pretty well with my depression overall. I am so grateful for all You have given me to overcome it, God. Thank You for the meds, for Dr. Smyth's helpful counseling, for the support group, for the books I read, for the people who have shared their pain and experience, for those who serve me during this time, for my victories. Thank You!!

June 25— Thank You, Lord, for counselors, for the insight and wisdom You have bestowed upon them to see into the lives of others. Thank You for Dr. Smyth and her help! It's amazing how You can use any of us, with all of our flaws. It's by grace we can be used by Him! Amen.

Cultivate an attitude of gratitude. I still find that writing down things that bring me joy or for which I am grateful moves my focus and brings more gratefulness into my life. These days, I typically do it each morning, including items from the previous day or things I am looking forward to on that day. For example, I have written down these types of things: hot apple cider, sunshine, a freezer stocked with food, tulips on my dining room table, time with my friends, and homemade potato soup.

From me to you

Giving thanks is not just for a day in November. When you list out blessings, however small or seemingly insignificant, your mood will shift. Some therapists recommend doing it at the end of each day, but any time of day is a good time for gratitude. Try it today and see how your mood improves.

Identify bad habits

July 1— Identifying bad habits again— I still struggle with excessive TV watching, though I know it's not as bad as it had been. But I am still wasting time there— cut out "Everybody Loves Raymond" and excessive game shows. None of the Hollywood "news" shows. Ask myself, "Do I really want to spend X time watching this? How could I better spend my time?" Sometimes I will want to watch it. Other times I can switch it off and listen to worship music instead. Another time waster is the internet. Sometimes I get sucked into email. I need to have a time limit when I sit down at the computer. Holy Spirit, help me in these two areas today and every day until it becomes natural for me. Amen

Nineteen years ago social media like we have today did not exist. Time was wasted in other ways. It's amazing to me that this can still be a struggle, probably even more so, two decades later! With easy access to the internet on our phones, it can be a real time waster if we're not careful! However, I did stop watching junk TV. That is a habit I was eventually able to break.

From me to you

Think about a bad habit you want to change. Can you commit to it? Ask a friend or your spouse to support you through accountability. Taking control in this area will help improve your mood, too.

Continuing struggles

July 10— Since I last wrote, I've had a few difficult days. Most recently when I was so overcome with anger over an unfair situation at the movie. I need to apologize for my behavior to the person who I sinned against, which won't be easy. I'm considering writing a letter, since I'm never going back to that theater. I was nearly bursting with my anger. I called Fiona and asked her to pray for me right then, which she did, and I was able to feel more peace as the day went on.

Today is my appointment with Dr. Smyth, my therapist. Brent is coming with me. I'm not sure how it will work, but I pray it will be positive for both of us and our marriage. Today I read Psalm 27— I will fear no one because the Lord is my light and the one who saves me. What a great Psalm.

I think I remember that situation at the movie theater. It was one of those free or cheap movies. They permitted too many people into the theater, but they did not tell us that until after we'd already purchased our concessions. I think I remember trying to sit on the floor because there were no seats. I was with my two kids and some friends. At that point we were told we couldn't sit on the floor due to fire regulations and would have to leave. My clear mind today understands that. That day, I was livid that they had overfilled the theater and sold us the snacks, but we couldn't stay to watch the show. I really made a scene. I can look back at PPD and see how it would be the start of my "mom anger" struggle. It took a decade for me to work through it and find a way out with God's help.

From me to you

When do you get angry? Can you see a pattern? Write about it in your journal. See Further Reading section for resources if that is an area in which you continue to struggle.

Excitement for life beyond PPD

Aug. 26— It's been so long since I've written! Feeling 100% better about PPD— stopped seeing my therapist with her blessing. Lost 20 pounds. Doing extremely well with my home party business.

I'm out to breakfast alone for the first time in a couple of months. Enjoying the beautiful weather outside at Panera Bread. Praying for a lot of different things including revival in my area. On Sunday, the pastor taught on making a difference for God with our lives by following Him and "swinging for the fence," as in hitting a homerun. He told us how our church is partnering with seven area churches and trying to bring others on board to lead to revival. Then I began to contemplate what my part is in all of this. And I feel led to pray for revival consistently. This is not something I would normally do, so I believe God is calling me to go above and beyond what I'll normally do. Wow! I am excited though. If I can play a role in bringing others to Jesus, I want to. Please use me Lord. Help me to swing for the fence in my daily life. Help me to please You in what I do, as I raise my kids, as I take care of my home, as I work my business, as I serve in church, as I interact with those around me, friends and others. I want to reflect Jesus in my daily life.

I have been enjoying my interaction on ww.com [Weight Watchers] as I'm losing weight. I've even gotten involved in a daily Christian challenge and shared with others what I am learning myself. I even started a group for new moms who need support losing their weight. I feel I am making a difference with people I will never meet. I ran into someone at a local Weight Watchers meeting that I went to college with. We both have seven-month-old girls and live in the same neighborhood. I am so glad I sat next to her. I feel that was from God for certain. I am reaching out more to neighbors and spending time with those who are not my best friends. This is not only good for me to expand my circle of friends and interact with other women, but it is good for Jesse. I know I need to be more intentional about teaching Jesse certain things, especially about moral upbringing. Once again I pray for the organization and discipline to be the mom I believe

You want me to be. I know I want to be more than I am now. I feel so inconsistent and like I'm floating through my day. I crave some schedule. Help me to make one and stick to it so I may be more effective in all of my roles.

More time had elapsed. It was the longest time between journal entries since prior to my PPD. I am disappointed as I look back and see I did not chronicle that month of getting better, though the journal was a tool I used only as needed. I do recall that once I started taking the Zoloft, things improved rapidly. About a week after the first dose, I remember feeling like a fog lifted from my mind. So much good came as a result of that, combined with the therapy, the support group, the self-help books, and Bible study and prayer.

From me to you

Can you see beyond your PPD right now? If not, do not lose hope. With help from doctors and counselors, you will get through this. Write in your journal what you would like your life to look like once you are seeing past the fog.

Feeling better

Sept. 12— God, I ask You to make me a stronger woman. Help me to have powers equal to my tasks. Ready me to do Your Will throughout my day. I have enjoyed ministering to others on the Weight Watchers community website, through encouragement and scripture. I pray You will continue to use me. Help me to reach out to "live" people too [in person, not on the internet].

There are many entries which follow, but they are simply prayers to God, unrelated to my PPD. I sometimes write out my prayers because I find it helpful to focus that way. This part of an entry jumped out at me though:

Oct. 2— I just went back and read some of the early pages in this journal. I was in a bad place indeed. Thank You, Lord, for bringing me through the PPD. I am grateful to feel so much better! To be a more improved me!

Again, I am grateful for the journal I kept during those dark months of PPD. I was able to look back and see how far I had come. I still journal all of the time, not daily but most days. It helps me to organize my thoughts and prayers and keep track of inspiration.

When does PPD end? Technically, it ends following the first year of the baby's life. My depression was limited to that time. If feelings of depression still persist, the doctors may shift the diagnosis to major depression. Continue to take your prescribed antidepressants, precisely as directed, and stay in counseling as needed.

From me to you

Journal entries do not have to be long or involved. Take time to journal about where you would like to be ten months from now.

Afterword

On January 28, 2021, my life changed direction. I was reading the devotional book *Live in Grace, Walk in Love* by Bob Goff. In that day's passage, Bob references Luke 18:27: "Jesus replied, 'What is impossible with man is possible with God.'" He writes about having a childlike faith, one that dreams, too. He also encourages readers to think about a dream they have set aside that it's time to pull out again.[14] I responded immediately, in my heart and then in my journal: "Writing. Writing for a living. God, show me what steps to take, how to do it and glorify you."

I spoke to some trusted family and friends about the dream, then I started slowly pursuing it, first signing up for Bob Goff's Dream Big writing course. That got me started. I worked through his *Dream Big* book and video course. Then these next two devotions in *Live in Grace, Walk in Love* guided me to finally put together the book you have just read.

In March 19th's entry, Bob writes that each person is telling a story with what she says or does.[15] In my journal I prayed, "God, may my story bring You glory. May it show You when held to the light." Then, in March 27th's entry, he writes that people just want to know they are not alone, that there is someone else who has been through what they are experiencing, to share the burden.[16] After reading those words, I knew without a doubt that God was calling me to pull out my old journal and start writing this memoir. It was time to share my experiences and, by doing so, help other women and their families who were experiencing PPD.

Yesterday my husband said to me that he remembered me telling him during my moments of clarity in the midst of PPD how I felt alone. He encouraged me by telling me perhaps my writing could help other women to know they were not alone. This just confirmed once again the title God gave me for this book.

Let me say it one last time: You are not alone. You will get through this. Look up and around. There are people who want to walk through this with you. Your Heavenly Father wants to draw you close and lift you out of your depression pit. Be vulnerable. Choose to remove yourself from the isolation, one step at a time. Find your safe people. Trust in God.

Appendix

Here is some more of God's Truth to help you see through the fog of your depression:

"Therefore encourage one another and build each other up, just as in fact you are doing." (1 Thessalonians 5:11)

"In the same way, the Spirit helps us in our weakness. We do not know what we ought to pray for, but the Spirit himself intercedes for us through wordless groans. And He who searches our hearts knows the mind of the Spirit, because the Spirit intercedes for God's people in accordance with the will of God." (Romans 8:26-27)

"Praise be to the God and Father of our Lord Jesus Christ, the Father of compassion and the God of all comfort, who comforts us in all our troubles, so that we can comfort those in any trouble with the comfort we ourselves receive from God." (2 Corinthians 1:3-4)

"So you have not received a spirit that makes you fearful slaves. Instead, you received God's Spirit when He adopted you as His own children. Now we call Him, 'Abba, Father.' For His Spirit joins with our spirit to affirm that we are God's children." (Romans 8:15-16 NLT)

"And we know that in all things God works for the good of those who love Him, who have been called according to His purpose." (Romans 8:28)

"May the God of hope fill you with all joy and peace as you trust in Him, so that you may over-flow with hope by the power of the Holy Spirit." (Romans 15:13)

"And the peace of God, which transcends all understanding, will guard your hearts and your minds in Christ Jesus." (Philippians 4:7)

"This is the confidence we have in approaching God: that if we ask anything according to His Will, He hears us." (I John 5:14)

"Consider it pure joy, my brothers and sisters, whenever you face trials of many kinds, because you know that the testing of your faith produces perseverance. Let perseverance finish its work so that you may be mature and complete, not lacking anything." (James 1:2-4)

"And I pray that you, being rooted and estab-lished in love, may have power, together with all the Lord's holy people, to grasp how wide and long and high and deep is the love of Christ, and to know this love that surpasses knowledge—that you may be filled to the measure of all the fullness of God." (Ephesians 3:17-19)

"O Lord, you are so good, so ready to forgive, so full of unfailing love for all who ask for your help." (Psalm 86:5 NLT)

Notes

Not alone

[1]: Resnick, Susan Kushner. *Sleepless Days: One Woman's Journey through Postpartum Depression*, 63. New York: St. Martin's Press, 2001.

Celebrate small victories

[2]: Dunnewold, Ann L., and Diane G. Sanford. *Postpartum Survival Guide*. Oakland, CA: New Harbinger Pub., 1995.

[3]: Sutton, Mark, and Bruce Hennigan. *Conquering Depression: A 30-Day Plan to Finding Happiness*. Nashville, TN: Broadman & Holman Publishers, 2001.

Finding comfort

[4]: Saavedra, Beth Wilson. *Meditations for New Mothers*, 5. London: Aquarian, 1993.

Thoughts and grief

[5]: Kleiman, Karen R., and Valerie D. Raskin. *This Isn't What I Expected: Recognizing and Recovering from Depression and Anxiety after Childbirth*, 26. New York: Bantam Books, 1994.

[6]: Kleiman, Karen R., and Valerie D. Raskin. *This Isn't What I Expected: Recognizing and Recovering from Depression and Anxiety after Childbirth*, 22. New York: Bantam Books, 1994.

Knowledge empowers
[7]: Kleiman, Karen R., and Valerie D. Raskin. *This Isn't What I Expected: Recognizing and Recovering from Depression and Anxiety after Childbirth*, 44. New York: Bantam Books, 1994.

Seek support
[8]: Kleiman, Karen R., and Valerie D. Raskin. *This Isn't What I Expected: Recognizing and Recovering from Depression and Anxiety after Childbirth*, 157. New York: Bantam Books, 1994.

Understand what you can control
[9]: Sutton, Mark, and Bruce Hennigan. *Conquering Depression: A 30-Day Plan to Finding Happiness*, 34-41. Nashville, TN: Broadman & Holman Publishers, 2001.

Being intentional
[10]: Sutton, Mark, and Bruce Hennigan. *Conquering Depression: A 30-Day Plan to Finding Happiness*, 95-100. Nashville, TN: Broadman & Holman Publishers, 2001.

Choosing to communicate
[11]: Sutton, Mark, and Bruce Hennigan. *Conquering Depression: A 30-Day Plan to Finding Happiness*, 95-100. Nashville, TN: Broadman & Holman Publishers, 2001.

Cling to God

[12]: Sutton, Mark, and Bruce Hennigan. *Conquering Depression: A 30-Day Plan to Finding Happiness*, 95-100. Nashville, TN: Broadman & Holman Publishers, 2001.

Big picture thinking

[13]: Lucado, Max. *The Inspirational Study Bible: Life Lessons from the Inspired Word of God*, 549. Dallas: Word Bibles, 1995.

Afterword

[14]: Goff, Bob. *Live in Grace, Walk in Love: A 365-Day Journey*, 36-37. Harpercollins Christian Pub, 2019.

[15]: Goff, Bob. *Live in Grace, Walk in Love: A 365-Day Journey*, 98. Harpercollins Christian Pub, 2019.

[16]: Goff, Bob. *Live in Grace, Walk in Love: A 365-Day Journey*, 111. Harpercollins Christian Pub, 2019.

Further Reading

Women's Moods: What Every Woman Must Know About Hormones, the Brain, and Emotional Health by Deborah Sichel, M.D., and Jeanne Watson Driscoll, M.S., R.N., C.S. was helpful for understanding the medical side of my experience.

Postpartum Survival Guide by Ann L. Dunnewold and Diane G. Sanford and *This Isn't What I Expected: Recognizing and Recovering from Depression and Anxiety after Childbirth* by Karen R. Kleiman and Valerie D. Raskin served to give practical, targeted help regarding PPD, its symptoms, and its treatments.

Conquering Depression: A 30-Day Plan to Finding Happiness by Mark Sutton and Bruce Hennigan served as a great devotional to meet both the spiritual and physical sides of my depression.

Meditations for New Mothers and *Meditations for Mothers of Toddlers* by Beth Wilson Saavedra were light devotional reads, the perfect kind to keep in the bathroom or in a basket for when you have a quiet moment.

Down Came the Rain: My Journey through Postpartum Depression by Brooke Shields is a first-person account of the actress' experience with PPD.

Sleepless Days: One Woman's Journey through Postpartum Depression by Susan Kushner Resnick provided insight into my experience during my early days of depression.

Good Moms Have Scary Thoughts: A Healing Guide to the Secret Fears of New Mothers and *What About Us?: A New Parents' Guide to Safeguarding Your Over-Anxious, Over-Extended, Sleep-Deprived Relationship,* both by Karen Kleiman, have been recommended as excellent resources for any new parents by Michelle Schaefer, LCPC. She also recommends the graphic novel memoir *Dear Scarlet: The Story of My Postpartum Depression* by Teresa Wong.

She's Gonna Blow! Real Help for Moms Dealing with Anger by Julie Ann Barnhill was a book I discovered when my kids were in preschool and early elementary. I read it many times to try to understand my anger issues relating to my kids.

Triggers: Exchanging Parents' Angry Reactions for Gentle Biblical Response by Amber Lia and Wendy Speake helped me to address the root behaviors regarding my anger and finally adopt new and healthy behaviors.

If you need help, here are some online resources, and full links can be found on my website at michelle habrych.com:

https://www.postpartum.net/learn-more/depression/

https://suicidepreventionlifeline.org/

Here is an online postpartum depression quiz: https://www.babycenter.com/baby/postpartum-health/postpartum-depression-quiz_20000530

If you would like help finding a counselor, here are some resources:

Better Help (https://www.betterhelp.com) offers online counseling.

Psychology Today's website (https://www.psychologytoday.com/us) has a "find a therapist" feature.

Postpartum Support International (PSI) offers a provider directory feature as well as connection to volunteers who could direct you to local support groups. PSI also has online support groups and a peer mentor program.

If you are looking for a moms group in your area to find support, many local churches host MOPS (Mothers of Preschoolers) groups. You may also be able to find other mom support groups, including support specifically for mothers who have had multiple babies at once (Mothers of Multiples, Mothers of Twins), by doing an internet search. Calling a local church may also be able to point you in the right direction.

Acknowledgements

This book came together as a result of much prayer and support, as well as the practical assistance of many people. First, if you prayed for this project, thank you! I remember the first time I talked about this project with a friend while walking at a forest preserve, praying it would be helpful to women experiencing postpartum depression. Knowing I had your support kept me going and on task.

Thank you everyone: To my husband, who allowed me to share our difficult story and encouraged me to persevere and finish writing this book. To my family, who saw me through the good and bad, who believed in this project and allowed the uninterrupted time to work on it. To my sister, who encouraged me to keep writing while we were on a road trip and kept telling me to Dream Big! To my friends, who asked how my project was progressing. To Michelle Schaefer, the first person to read the rough manuscript and encourage me— thank you for your patience with all of my questions! To my beta readers Pam, Lynda, Val, Chrissi, Liz, Rachel, Kara, Cindy, Katie, and Alice, who gave honest and helpful feedback to make this book better than it was before their suggestions. To my friend Rachel Fahrenbach, for introducing me to hope*writers, a community of writers which made finishing this project possible, and for answering my questions about self-publishing. To my hope*writers friends who walked through the self-publishing process with me: Carrie, Ruth, Angela, and Aimee, I wouldn't be here without the accountability and guidance our group provided— I wish you all the best in your publishing journeys. To Faith, Chrissi, and Elizabeth, for providing an extra set of eyes to edit this manuscript and offering suggestions to make it even better.

I would not be able to finish without thanking God for bringing me through this process so I could bring beauty from the ashes. Thank You, Lord, for using my experience to encourage others.

About the Author

Reading and writing have been part of my life, as far back as I can remember. Whether it was curling up with a *Nancy Drew* book, writing an adventure story featuring my stuffed animals, or creating a newsletter for my friends on my family's first home computer, I wanted to be involved with the written word. The first article I wrote for the school newspaper was a review of the brand-new TV show, "ALF." Seeing my byline was an unmatched thrill. I was hooked.

High school and college writing prepared me for a career in journalism. With my degree in communication from the College of Lake County, I spent a year both reporting for a small town weekly newspaper and editing three of the other local papers my employer published. I enjoyed this career very much before my husband and I began our family in 2001.

Two decades later, after homeschooling both of our children, I am drawn back to writing as my life's passion. Encouraged by motivational speaker and author Bob Goff, I am dreaming big and working on writing projects which mean something special to me. I am a hope*writer, a member of the Historical

Novel Society, and a member of the Women's Fiction Writers Association.

I live in the Chicagoland area with my husband and best friend of 26 years, as well as our two college-age kids. In my free time, I enjoy putting together puzzles, playing board games, cheering for the Chicago Bears football team, and, of course, reading and discussing books.

Connect with Michelle

michellehabrych.com
facebook.com/MichelleHabrych
michellehabrych@gmail.com